DO YOU KNOW

AEROPLANES

From
AerMacchi to Zlin

Compiled by
IAN WILSON

Edited by
FRANCIS COOKE

POCKET REFERENCE BOOKS

A POCKET REFERENCE BOOK

Published by:
Pocket Reference Books Publishing Ltd.
Premier House
Hinton Road
Bournemouth
Dorset BH1 2EF

First published 1996

Typesetting:	Gary Tomlinson PrintRelate (Bournemouth, Dorset) (01202) 897659
Cover Design:	Van Renselar Bonney Design Associates West Wickham, Kent BR4 9QH
Illustrations	John Warren
Printing and Binding:	RPM Reprographics Units 2-3 Spur Road Quarry Lane, Chichester West Sussex PO19 2PR Tel. 01243 787077 Fax. 01243 780012 Modem 01243 536482 E-Mail: rpm@argonet.co.uk

ISBN: 1 899437 00 2

A POCKET REFERENCE BOOK

Contents	**Pages**

ALL POCKET REFERENCE BOOKS INCLUDE A
FREE FULL PAGE ADVERTISEMENT ON THE
INSIDE FRONT COVER FOR A WELL-KNOWN CHARITY
SELECTED BY THE AUTHOR

THE HISTORY OF THE CHARITY IS INCLUDED ON
THE INSIDE BACK COVER

The Publishers cannot be held responsible for any omissions or
information which is incorrect.

A very wide range of sources has been used by the compiler and the
editor, and the content of this Pocket Reference Book is dependent upon
the accuracy of those sources.

INTRODUCTION

On December 8th 1903 the future of the aeroplane looked bleak.

Pioneer Samuel Langley's flying machine had plunged into a river within moments of launch, for the second time. One newspaper writer predicted that it would be a million years before heavier-than-air flight was achieved.

Forecasting is notoriously risky, but it was to be just nine days before the Wright brothers confounded that prophesy. Even the Wrights would probably have thought it far-fetched to suppose that within a mere 36 years, fare-paying passengers would cross the Atlantic by air. Nor could they have foreseen that in the same year a little aeroplane would herald a revolution in aeronautics, for it was in 1939 that the first jet flew.

Alas, within days a war would begin which would show another side to aviation, its fearsome destructive capability.

In another 36 years transatlantic passengers who so chose and could afford the fare (or more usually persuade their employers to pay it) could cross that ocean at twice the speed of sound. Yet it is not supersonic travel which has so much changed the world.

Far more important have been the astounding improvements in economics and safety. It is now possible to cross the Atlantic for a lower fare than in 1939, distant lands are within reach of people of quite modest means as never before and airline flying has become far safer per mile than travelling by car.

This book tells how the most significant types played their part in aviation history and shows their good and bad points. It is not a technical book and does not list a mass of engineering data on matters such as engine powers or take-off weights. The selection of types will be controversial, but since more readers are likely to be newcomers to the topic than lifetime professionals, emphasis is on the more interesting ones.

Thus a few interesting failures are here while some not very exciting business aircraft and feederliners are omitted. Helicopters are limited to the most historically important, for on the whole they are of specialised interest (and not everyone counts them as 'aeroplanes' anyway!).

Reluctantly excluded are all but a handful of light aircraft and sailplanes. It must always be remembered that an aeroplane is a machine. It was not the Hurricane and Spitfire which won the Battle of Britain, nor the Vimy which flew the Atlantic; that credit belongs to their courageous crews and the designers and builders behind the scenes.

Listing is alphabetical, first by maker's name, then by type, name or number. This does lose chronological sequence, so a modern jet may precede a biplane, but it should be easy enough to find a given type once the maker is known. Herein lies another problem. Due to mergers the maker's name often changes during the lifetime of an aeroplane – the most popular British business jet has been sold under five manufacturers' names! The practice adopted is to list under the original designing company. An index is provided to help in locating types.

IAN WILSON

TEASERS

When was the speed of sound first reached?

Who designed an aeroplane to be flown from a submarine?

Which was the first jet aircraft to fly?

When was the largest aeroplane in the world made in Scotland?

Which First World War British type was still flying in 1940?

Which aeroplane builder was a pioneer maker of ball-point pens?

When was the first flight over Mount Everest?

Which was the most widely used American bomber of World War Two?

Which airliner has been carrying passengers for 60 years?

Whose airliner featured an outside promenade deck?

How did the Lancaster emerge from a failure?

Which British wartime bomber was designed by a German?

Why was the first American jet fitted with a propeller?

Which helicopter was called the 'flying banana'?

Why did some Flying Fortress bombers carry no bombs?

What took 12 engines and $9^1/2$ months to cross the Atlantic?

How did an aerobatic pilot land safely with a broken wing?

What was the only rocket-propelled aeroplane to see service?

Which was the second jet airliner to fly?

Whose 1921 100-passenger airliner crashed on its first flight?

Which German fighter began and ended life on Rolls-Royce power?

Which early airliner had windows in the floor?

How did American crews frighten the Japanese with beer bottles?

Which large transport has been made for forty years?

Why were some round Douglas airliner windows painted square?

Which aeroplane was unsymmetrical if seen head-on?

Which jet fighter was designed, built and flown in three months?

How did a slow biplane cripple the battleship Bismarck?

Which propeller-driven aircraft has sharply swept wings?

Which Rolls-Royce jet engine was widely used in Russia?

(You will find the answers to these teasers in the following pages)

AerMacchi Mb326 and 339
Jet trainers and light strike aircraft for the world

The Italian Macchi company is one of the oldest aeroplane builders in the world. Guilio Macchi started in 1912, at first making French Nieuports but soon progressing to his own designs. The firm has traded under the AerMacchi name since 1962 although still registered as Macchi.

Macchi was famed for its seaplanes in the 1920s and 1930s. Several world speed records were held and Macchis were among the main contenders for the Schneider Trophy races for marine aircraft.

The principal Italian fighter of World War Two was the 1937 Macchi MC200 Saetta, but it was outclassed against top Allied machines. The firm rose again after the war and became highly successful, thanks largely to talented designer Ermanno Bazzocchi. His Mb326 jet trainer, first flown in 1957, became one of the most successful in its class.

It was built not only in Italy but also in South Africa, Australia, and Brazil. The Mb339 is a modernised and more powerful version, built both as a trainer and as a light strike-aircraft. It, too, has sold well, especially to countries unable to afford the fearsome cost of the highest performance combat aircraft.

Like many other firms, AerMacchi is now much involved in international projects, notably as part of an Italian/Brazilian group building a more advanced strike aircraft called the AMX. Nowadays military aircraft are so expensive few firms and even countries can build them alone.

THE GREAT LITTLE VIPER

The Viper engine used in the Mb326 and 339 is a little-known success story. The Armstrong Siddeley Viper (now part of the Rolls-Royce stable) was designed in the early 1950s as a "throw- away" engine for an unmanned (naturally!) Australian target aeroplane called the Jindivik.

Soon it was realised that a more durable version would be ideal for jet trainers and it has been widely used for that purpose throughout the world. Later it powered large numbers of business jets, until the need for quieter and more economical engines displaced it. However, in trainers new applications are still appearing.

Some 5,500 Vipers have been made over 40 years – possibly the longest time any aero-engine has remained in production other than those for light aircraft only – an impressive achievement for an engine originally intended to last just a few hours!

Airbus airliners

the European triumph which confounded the 'experts'

In the early 1960s various European companies started joint design studies on large, efficient, twin-engine 'wide-body' airliners. A firm proposal was settled in 1966 as the A300, for 'Airbus, 300 seats'.

The British, French and German governments signed an agreement to proceed in 1967, but two years later the British government pulled out after having one of its recurring attacks of cold feet involving aviation projects. Hawker Siddeley continued as a sub contractor, designing the wings (the efficiency of which has contributed much to the Airbus success), but many British firms lost a great opportunity.

The A300 was launched as the smaller 250-seat A300B (the notion of using the type number to show the number of seats did not last long!). First flight was on 28th October 1972 and it entered service with Air France in 1974. Engines were General Electric CF6-50s or Pratt and Whitney JT9Ds.

Soon the A300B built up an excellent name for low fuel cost and reliability, but would it sell? Many doubted it. How would an unknown newcomer compete with the long-established American airliner builders? In 1976 just one Airbus was sold. It looked as though the doubters were right, but then came the turning-point: Eastern Airlines, one of the largest American carriers, leased four Airbuses, found them highly efficient and placed large orders.

Airbus has gone from strength to strength ever since. Now the consortium followed up their success by expanding their range, adding the long-range A300-600 and the smaller 210-240 seat A310 which started service in 1983. A totally new design was the 250-seat A320, a 'single-aisle' layout, unlike the others which are 'wide-bodies'. It broke new ground in airliner design in using 'fly-by-wire' controls, with no mechanical linkage between cockpit and control surfaces, and large colour cockpit displays instead of traditional dials. Pilots entering the A320 also notice something else – there is no control column! Instead there are small 'sidestick controllers' beside the seats.

The airliner can almost fly a route itself with the pilot keeping an eye on proceedings, but two highly publicised accidents, one at an air display, showed that like any aeroplane it must be handled with respect. Engines on the A320 are either the CFM56, jointly built by the French company SNECMA and General Electric, or the V2500 built by a group including Rolls-Royce, Pratt and Whitney, German and Japanese companies. Aviation is truly international now!

Still the Airbus range expands, with the twin-engine A330 as successor to the A300B and the four-engine A340 which ingeniously shares the same wing, cockpit and tail. For the first time on an Airbus, a Rolls-Royce engine, the Trent, is offered on the A330.

The thousandth Airbus was delivered in 1993 and the group (which now includes Spanish and Dutch companies) now rivals Boeing for world leadership in jet airliner sales.

> *Early in the Airbus project it was the British minister involved who worked tirelessly to 'sell' the idea to the other countries and who must take some credit for the Airbus success.*
>
> *Later he was to become famous for a less creditable reason. He faked his own death and disappeared, later to be found in Australia with a lady companion. His name was John Stonehouse.*

Airco DH4 and DH9
outstanding light bombers of the First World War

The Aircraft Manufacturing Company, or Airco, was founded by George Holt Thomas in 1912. Astutely he employed the great pioneer Geoffrey de Havilland as his designer, hence the 'DH' in the aircraft numbers. The first successful design was the DH2, a 'pusher' biplane with the gunner in the nose. Some 200 were built and served well before becoming outclassed.

However it was the DH4 single-engine biplane light bomber which won renown for Airco and its designer. First flown by 'DH' himself in 1916, the DH4 proved fast and capable. It is widely held to have been one of the best light bombers of the war. Various engines were used but the most popular was the Rolls-Royce Eagle.

One drawback with the DH4 was that pilot and gunner were separated by the fuel tank and were unable to speak to each other. The fuel tank location also gave the aeroplane the grim name of 'flying coffin'. 1,450 DH4s were built in Britain but no less than 4,844 in America, with Liberty engines. Indeed the DH4 was the most numerous type in American service at the time.

For a decade after the war it was the mainstay of the pioneering American airmail services. Back in Britain, modified DH4s were used for early airline services, but the small passenger capacity made for poor economics and such services were short-lived.

The DH9 was a supposedly improved version which entered service in 1918. Due to a shortage of Eagle engines, Siddeley Pumas were generally used, and it soon became clear that performance was worse than that of the DH4. However at least the cockpit layout now allowed the two crew to communicate.

A much better version was the DH9a, or 'Nine-ack', with American Liberty engines. It became a major element in the post-war RAF for a decade. It was largely with the DH9a that the RAF pioneered the use of airpower in keeping dissident troublemakers in order, notably in the Middle East, then as now a perpetual area of friction. A few aeroplanes could contain a problem that would otherwise need hundreds of ground troops.

The DH9a continued in service until 1932. Airco closed with the loss of wartime business, but Geoffrey de Havilland formed his own company and continued the long line of 'DH' designs.

Airspeed Oxford
standard wartime twin-engine trainer

Airspeed was formed by Hessell Tiltman and Neville Shute Norway (the novellist Neville Shute) in the early 1930s. The Oxford story starts with the single-engine Courier of 1933, the first British aircraft to enter production with a retractable undercarriage.

At the time it was a daring innovation, for many thought the gains would not justify the weight and complexity, but the Courier proved them wrong with its excellent performance. A twin-engine version, the Envoy, followed, and with it the little company secured a coup when it was selected for the King's Flight.

The Envoy was also built under licence in Japan. The Envoy was further developed into the military Oxford, not one of the front-line glamour aeroplanes but still a most important contributor to the war effort. It became a standard twin-engine, navigation, and gunnery trainer for the Empire Air Training Scheme, whereby crew training took place well away from combat zones. Most pilots of larger aircraft would have handled an Oxford at some stage.

8,751 were built. Engines were Armstrong Siddeley Cheetahs or Pratt & Whitney Wasp Juniors. Some were converted to civil use as the Consul, a few flying until 1960. Airspeed's other major wartime product was the standard British troop-carrying glider, the Horsa, used by the hundreds in the Arnhem and Rhine landings.

After the war Airspeed built the high-wing, twin-engine Ambassador airliner of 1947. By then Airspeed was part of de Havilland and a combination of other priorities in the parent company and the coming of the turbine Viscount limited sales of this outstandingly beautiful airliner to 20 for the state airline BEA.

> *Airspeed made a pilotless radio-controlled target biplane, the Queen Wasp. On landing, a trailing wire touched the ground, shut off the engine, and raised the elevators. On one approach the radio controller brought it too low and the wire caught on trees.*
> *Personnel poured out from buildings for, it was related, "nothing could attract a crowd faster than the sight of an aeroplane about to crash with no risk of anyone being hurt!" The Queen Wasp obliged with a spectacular bonfire.*

Albatros fighter
leading German fighters of World War One

The Albatros series appeared in mid-1916. The company had managed virtually to corner the supply of Mercedes 160 hp engines, at the time the best in Germany. The Albatros fighters therefore offered the highest performance available to German pilots and many of the country's 'aces' scored their victories on these machines. However, some wing failures led to restrictions on diving, and by 1918 even the latest of the Albatros series were becoming outclassed.

Antoinette
elegant early French monoplanes

The creator of the Antoinettes, Léon Levavasseur, conceived the idea of building an aeroplane as early as 1902. He started by building a lightweight engine with extensive use of aluminium which he called 'Antoinette' after the daughter of his financial backer.

Antoinette engines were used first in power-boats, then for a time became almost the standard power unit for European aviation pioneers. The first successful Antoinette aeroplanes appeared in 1908.

These monoplanes have always been considered to have been exceptionally graceful for their day and were flown by many early French pilots. Sadly the direct injection engine was vulnerable to any impurities in the fuel and twice let the Anglo-French pilot Hubert Latham down into the English Channel, losing the chance for Antoinette to achieve fame with the first crossing.

Although advanced in 1908, Antoinettes later lost their prominent position and the company had disappeared by 1914.

The famous trailblazing pilot Alan Cobham was flying a DH9 to parachute films of the 1922 Derby race to waiting motorcyclists who were to carry them to cinemas for showing the same day. One parachute caught on his tailskid but later fell free.

On landing he was congratulated on his extraordinary skill It had landed in the yard of the cinema where it was destined!

Antonov An-2 Antek
the biplane which has outsold every monoplane

The An-2 biplane may have looked an anachronism when it appeared in 1947, but Antonov had conceived one of the most remarkable aeroplanes in history, for it is still being made in the 1990s!

The versatile machine has been used as a small airliner, for freight carrying, crop-spraying and almost any form of aerial work. While in the West single-engine airliners would no longer be acceptable, over the wide open spaces of the Eastern countries they still have their place, and until recently Russian passengers would have been ill-advised to complain!

Some 5,000 were made by Antonov before production was moved to the present source in Poland, which has built a further 10,000. Since 1957 the biplane has also been built in China and possibly continues. The production span approaching 50 years is likely to be a record for any aircraft and the total of over 15,000 built is also a peacetime record (excluding light aircraft).

Antonov An-22 Antheus
Russia's heavyweight lifter

In a country where many areas are inaccessible to surface transport, large air freighters are invaluable. Antonov had already designed some tough freighters, the An-10 and An-12, similar in layout and duties to the Western workhorse, the Lockheed Hercules.

The An-22 was on a bigger scale, for when it appeared in 1965 it was considered the largest aircraft in the world. Its 211ft (64m) span wing enables the An-22 to carry over 80 tons and it has held a number of world payload records.

Arado 234 Blitz
first jet bomber

This was a remarkably advanced aeroplane when it entered service in July 1944, rivalling the Gloster Meteor and Me 262 as the first jet in service. The honours are generally given to the Meteor, but it is difficult to define precisely when a type is 'in service'.

The two Junkers Jumo 004B engines gave the 234 a speed of 460mph (740 kph). A four-engine version was also built. About 300 were made, being used either as bombers or for photographic reconnaissance.

Armstrong Whitworth airliners
from Argosy to Argosy

The first Argosy was a 20-passenger trimotor biplane first flown in 1926. The seven built were the first Imperial Airways airliners to be profitable and gave reliable, even if noisy and draughty, service for nine years with one fatal accident.

The 1932 Atalaya four-engine monoplane looked advanced for its time, and the eight built served well, some flying as late as 1944.

The 1938 Ensign was much larger and looked impressive, but was handicapped by being underpowered with its four Armstrong Siddeley Tiger engines, which were further noted for poor reliability. Some of the 14 Ensigns were re-engined with Wright Cyclones during the war.

After the war the company designed an elegant turboprop airliner, the Apollo, but it was abandoned when the Viscount took the launch orders for BEA. The company's last transport was the 1959 Argosy freighter, a high-wing twin tail-boom design with four Rolls-Royce Dart engines.

A large RAF order and a promising sale to an America cargo airline, Riddle, set the Argosy off to an encouraging start, but few other civil sales were secured.

Armstrong Whitworth

Siskin III – first RAF metal fighter

Biplanes tend to be associated with wood and fabric, but this metal aeroplane entered service as long ago as 1924. The Armstrong Siddeley Jaguar engine was supercharged, the first such production installation in the world. The highly aerobatic Siskin was a mainstay of RAF fighter squadrons until 1932.

Armstrong Whitworth Whitley

British wartime medium bomber

First flown in 1936, the Whitley was to be one of the principal RAF bombers in the early part of the war, although by then it was already outmoded. Engines were two Armstrong Siddeley Tigers, or more satisfactorily, Rolls-Royce Merlins.

1,814 Whitleys were built. By 1941 they were being superceded as bombers but many continued in service as glider tugs, in which role they had one moment of glory for their part in the famous commando raid capturing a German radar at Bruneval.

An intended successor, the Albemarle, was really obsolete by the time it was ready for service and was likewise relegated for glider-towing. Its sole claim to fame is in being the first RAF British operational aircraft with a tricycle undercarriage.

TAILS UP!

The Whitley is probably best known for its strange trait of flying perpetually nose-down. The reason for this is that the wing was designed without flaps, although they were later added, so to assist landing, the wings were set at an angle to the fuselage (angle of incidence), leading to the nose-down cruise.

Austers

British light aircraft family

The long line of Austers started shortly before World War Two as licence-built American Taylorcraft designs. During the war they were widely used by the army as Air Observation Posts (AOP), spotting where artillery fire was falling and radioing back corrections – needless to say a most hazardous duty as the other side did not take kindly to this activity.

Austers continued in a similar role in Malaya and Korea. Nowadays this task is handled by helicopters. Many Austers were used as civil light aircraft in the 1940s and 1950s, until displaced by modern American types.

Auster was absorbed in 1960 into Beagle, the group which was supposed to rejuvenate British light aeroplane building. It didn't.

Avro 504
classic trainer of the biplane era

Thousands of pilots learned to fly in Avro's Classic 504

The Avro 504 was made for over 20 years, spanning the period before World War One well into the age of metal monoplanes. The origins of Avro go back to 1909, when on 13th July its founder, Alliott Verdon Roe made the first flight in a British aeroplane.

That was in a triplane with a puny 9hp JAP engine. Not everyone applauded his pioneering achievements. His local council tried to prosecute him for 'causing a public nuisance'. Roe was far-sighted, and is credited with being the first to use a single control for pitch and bank, and the first to fly an aircraft with an enclosed cabin, his 1912 Type F monoplane.

The Avro 500 was built in 1911 to meet the first ever War Office specification for a military aeroplane. The 504 was an improved version, first flown in 1913. In the war to come the 504 was used for every conceivable duty, as a 'scout', a rudimentary fighter with a machine-gun fixed to the upper wing, as a bomber, and in its most famous role as a trainer. Who claimed the multi-role combat aircraft was a new idea when the 1970s Tornado appeared?.

Three machines made what is regarded as the first strategic bombing raid in history, on the Zeppelin sheds at Friedrichshaven in November 1914. Some damage was caused.

With well harmonised controls and full aerobatic ability, the 504 made an ideal trainer and became the standard machine for the RFC and later RAF.

Over 5,000 were built, including some in Russia; some sources quote Avro 504 production as over 8,000. Various engines were used, the most popular being the Gnome Monosoupape rotary, giving the 504 its characteristic smell of castor oil and staccato sound as the pilot 'blipped' the engine to reduce power – the 'blip' switch cut the power momentarily as there was no throttle.

After the war the 504 remained in use as a trainer, and indeed improved versions were built with the Armstrong Siddeley Lynx engine up until 1932 in Britain and as late as 1937 overseas. War-surplus aircraft were widely used by 'barnstorming' display pilots and for joyriding with as many as four passengers crammed into the rear cockpit. Modern airworthiness authorities would not approve!

A few Avro 504s were still flying with the RAF in the Second World War, for duties such as radar testing, so this remarkable aeroplane was one of the very few to fly in both world wars.

FIRST FLIGHTS

In an era when air travel was still a rarity, 'barnstorming' pilots with their Avro 504s brought a first taste of flight to thousands, but those pilots worked hard for their living – some flew over 40 times a day, and one, Percival Phillips, carried 91,000 passengers in his trusty 504.

Avro airliners
from failure to world-wide success

Until the Second World war, Avro had concentrated on military and light aircraft, although they had dabbled in airliners with the 1928 Avro Ten, a modified Fokker trimotor.

14 were built, one called 'Southern Cloud' becoming the centre of a famous mystery when it disappeared without trace in Australia in 1931.

During the war Avro built a transport version of the Lancaster called the York. One was used by Winston Churchill. The workmanlike York served well for many years, including carrying 250,000 tons of cargo in the Berlin Airlift. An even cruder adaptation of the Lancaster was the long-range Lancastrian, which launched early post-war airline services to Australia and Canada, although with just 9 or 12 passengers it did little for airline profits.

The great post-war hope was the Tudor, designed as an airliner from scratch. Surely under the design of the famous Roy Chadwick this would put Britain back into airliner leadership? Alas it was not to be. The first version carried 12 passengers on the power of four Rolls-Royce Merlin engines. Douglas and Lockheed airliners held 50 on similar engine power. Inevitably it did not sell. The message was taken and an enlarged version seated 60.

The prototype crashed on take-off killing Roy Chadwick and test pilot Bill Thorn. The ailerons had been connected in reverse. Tudors did enter service with a few airlines but their troubles were far from over. Two, Star Tiger and Star Aeriel, disappeared over the North Atlantic. Another crashed near Cardiff, probably due to loading error, killing all on board.

The airliner served well on the Berlin Airlift and some gave respectable service as freighters for some years, but their reputation was too tarnished to realise their maker's original hopes. To some extent, Avro were perhaps rather unlucky with the Tudor – some crews regarded it highly.

Avro kept away from airliners for some years after their problems with the Tudor, but when they did return to the market they produced a winner, the 50-seat twin Rolls-Royce Dart powered Avro 748, first flown in 1960. It sold well throughout the world and was also built in India. Over most of its life it was sold as the Hawker Siddeley and later British Aerospace 748, reflecting changed ownership of the company.

Around 440 were sold. An RAF freighter version with large rear loading ramp was called the Andover. An unusual feature was that the height of the nosewheel could be altered on the ground to ease loading – the so-called 'kneeling undercarriage'. 'Andovers' were also used by the Queen's Flight, but here the name was a misnomer for they were closer to the airline 748.

By the mid-1980s the Dart engine was becoming dated and inefficient (what a pity Rolls-Royce never made a successor!), and a new version, the clumsily named BAe ATP (Advanced Turboprop) was launched, using Pratt and Whitney engines, with only moderate success. In the 1990s it was updated again as the BAe Jetstream 61, a most confusing name as 'Jetstream' is the name of the former Handley Page feederliner also built by British Aerospace.

Equally confusingly, the Avro name now flies again. The British Aerospace 'RJ' (Regional Jets) series of airliners such as RJ70 and RJ100 now bear the Avro name. The irony is that they were originally designed by de Havilland! Aviation today is complex!

THE CASE OF THE DISAPPEARING AVROS

The mysterious disappearances of Southern Cloud, Star Tiger and Star Aeriel have intrigued writers for decades. There is actually no mystery about Southern Cloud. The weather was so violent that the crew were rash to depart. Many crews still felt honour-bound to keep to the wartime 'press-on' spirit regardless of conditions, although it was not really appropriate to carrying passengers. The wreckage was finally found in 1958.

Whatever happened to the Tudors must have been sudden, for there were no distress messages. Were there failures of the structure, or of the radio, or a cabin heater explosion? Some have blamed a supposedly sinister 'Bermuda Triangle', for Star Tiger was descending to the island and Star Aeriel had left it. Or was a perfectly serviceable airliner flown into the sea? With the 'three-pointer' altimeters of the day a tired crew could misread the tiny 10,000ft needle and hit the ground or sea before they were even aware of danger.

The truth will probably never be known. Or will it? Such is the fascination of this mystery of the air that in 1994 an expedition was announced to find Star Tiger.

It is not unusual for pilots to form an affection for their aircraft. One Avro 504 pilot in 1917 took this to extremes in christening his son 'Avro'. Unfortunately so many people thought Avro must be a girl's name that the family later called him a more conventional 'John'.

> *Several pilots giving joy rides felt one of their number was being mean to his passengers by giving them excessively short flights. When their hints were ignored, two of them flew in such close formation on either side of the offender that he was unable to turn and was forced to prolong the flight.*
>
> *Whether his passengers on that flight appreciated it or were frightened out of their wits is not recorded!*

Avro Anson
the 'Faithful Annie' which served the RAF for 32 years

The Anson started as a light airliner, the Avro 652 which first flew in 1935 and served with Imperial Airways. The Anson entered RAF service in 1936 as a coastal patrol aeroplane. For the RAF it broke new ground in being their first monoplane and their first with a retractable undercarriage. This feature was not appreciated by all crews – early versions needed 140 turns of a handle to raise the wheels!

The Anson was outmoded in its original duty by the time war broke out, although some crews achieved remarkable successes in beating off enemy attacks. The Anson really came into its own as a trainer for twin-engine conversions, navigation, and gunnery. Many were also used as light transports and as air ambulances.

10,996 Ansons were built, most with two Armstrong Siddeley Cheetah engines of around 350 hp, although those made in Canada used American engines. Many Ansons were used after the war by small airlines, but by 1960 deterioration of glued joints brought their flying days to an end.

The last Ansons in RAF service flew on until 1968, ending a long and distinguished career for an aeroplane always well liked by all who flew her.

Lancaster
the outstanding wartime heavy night bomber

One of the most famous of military aeroplanes, the Lancaster started life as the Manchester with two Rolls-Royce Vulture engines. This complex 24-cylinder engine was a rare failure for the company and during the bomber's short operational history from 1940 till 1942, many aircraft and crews were lost due to engine problems.

Few mourned the passing of the Manchester. Designer Roy Chadwick transformed the Manchester by fitting four Merlin engines. In case Merlins became in short supply, one version used the Bristol Hercules. To break the link with its unpopular ancestor, the new bomber was renamed Lancaster.

First flight was on 9th January 1941 and operations started early in 1942. The Lancaster became the most important RAF heavy bomber. It carried a far heavier load than any other (about triple that of the Boeing B-17 Flying Fortress) and was well liked by crews for its handling and strength – some pilots reportedly looped them!

Over 150,000 Lancaster missions were flown for a loss rate of around 2½% per raid. If that sounds low, which it is compared with some bombers, work out the odds over the quota of 50 missions. No less than 10 Lancaster crew members earned V.C.s. Famous raids included the 'Dambusters' success in breaching two major dams in May 1943, that on the V-weapons testing site at Peenemünde, and sinking the battleship Tirpitz.

Avro Lancaster – Mightiest War-time Night Bomber

Some precision attacks used the 10-ton 'Grand Slam' bomb, the heaviest of that war. 7,377 Lancasters were built, the last RAF examples being retired in 1954. An improved version with a longer wing, the Lincoln, was the last RAF piston-engine bomber.

Avro Shackleton
Britain's airborne 'eyes' for 40 years

The Shackleton was a maritime reconnaissance development of the Lincoln with a more spacious fuselage and four Rolls-Royce Griffon engines. It first flew in 1949. As well as watching for hostile ships and submarines, Shackletons were used searching for survivors of disasters at sea, and how welcome must they have been to those awaiting rescue.

If need be a Shackleton could patrol for 24 hours, at some cost in crew fatigue – a complaint of hearing difficulty was called 'Griffon ear'! More and more equipment was added over the years, so much so that some were fitted with two Viper jet engines to help on take-off. The only overseas sale was to South Africa, where they served for 28 years until grounded by British government spares restrictions.

A number of Shackletons were adapted for Airborne Early Warning radar duties. Due to delays to their intended successors the Shackletons continued until 1992, when this last link with the Lancaster finally took its well-earned retirement.

> *The elderly Early Warning Shackletons bore names such as 'Florence', 'Dougal', and 'Dill' from children's television series. A new commanding officer objected to juvenile names and had them removed. On his departure air- and ground-crews, fond of these fine old aeroplanes, had them restored and preserved Shackletons once more bear these names.*

> *Like many firms, Auster published a newsletter for its customers. A report on an Auster changing hands mentioned that this example had been the first aeroplane used in a murder, when Donald Hulme had dropped the dismembered remains of his victim over marshes.*
> *The newsletter unwisely continued "we are always pleased to hear of Austers continuing to do good work....."*

Avro Vulcan
the mighty delta

Avro designer Stuart Davies took the bold step of using a delta wing (named after the shape of the Greek capital letter 'delta') to meet an RAF requirement for a four-engine jet bomber. Prudently the company flew some small delta research aircraft, the Avro 707s, from 1949 onwards to test the design.

The Vulcan itself first flew on 30th August, 1952, at the hands of 'Roly' Falk. This futuristic-looking bomber created a sensation the following month at the Farnborough Show. Even more sensationally, three years later Falk performed a slow roll at low level at the show.

136 Vulcans were built. All production aircraft used Bristol Olympus engines, initially of around 11,000 pounds thrust but eventually doubling this power. Five crew were carried, but inconsistently only the front two had ejector seats. One brave captain delayed his escape so long to give his rear crew a chance that he only survived because his partly opened parachute caught in overhead wires.

From 1957 till 1969 Vulcans formed the British nuclear deterrent force. As Soviet defences improved, Vulcans were fitted with the Blue Steel rocket-propelled 'stand-off' bomb, which could be launched 200 miles (320km) from the target. Vulcans on 'quick-reaction alert' could be airborne within four minutes.

In 1982 Vulcans were used 'in anger' for the only time in bombing the Argentine-held airfield at Port Stanley in the Falkland Islands. The 7,800 mile round trip from Ascension Island made these flights the longest bombing raids in history and involved no less than 10 Victor tankers per mission. Victors had to refuel each other for the more distant 'prods'. On the first raid a direct hit was scored on the runway.

The Vulcan was one of the most impressive aeroplanes ever to fly. Even hardened aviation professionals marvelled at the great deltas climbing and turning like outsize fighters – indeed they could out-turn almost any fighter.

There was a practical value too in its awesome appearance. A flight of Vulcans overhead a tiresome dictator stirring up trouble soon reminded him that Britain was still a power in the world. It is no wonder so many aspire to flying once more one of these fine machines, although the difficulties may prove insurmountable.

> *The crew of an American owned Argosy freighter were low on fuel and elected to land on a freeway (motorway). Unluckily a bridge had a shorter span than an Argosy so the crew ended up with a wingless aeroplane, but no-one was hurt.*

Avro Canada CF100
Excellent Canadian fighter

The twin-engine all-weather CF100 flew in 1950 and proved one of the finest of its time. 692 were built for Canada and Belgium, serving until 1962. Engines were Avro Canada Orendas. An intended successor, the CF105 Arrow, flew in 1958 but was cancelled the next year.

Avro Canada also built the second jet transport in the world, the CF102 Jetliner, which flew in August 1949, shortly after the Comet. The straight-winged airliner was powered by four Rolls-Royce Derwent engines. Only the prototype was completed.

Beagle (later Scottish Aviation) Bulldog
light military trainer

The Beagle company was formed by a merger of the remnants of various British light aeroplane makers in the hope of reviving a field in which Britain had once done so well. For various reasons those hopes foundered, but one design, the Beagle Pup and its military offshoot the Bulldog were deemed so good that the latter was put into production by Scottish Aviation.

The Bulldog first flew in 1969 and is used in large numbers by the RAF and a few overseas customers as a primary trainer, being particularly noted for its aerobatic handling.

Beardmore Inflexible
Scotland's giant

The shipbuilding firm of William Beardmore was a major producer of aircraft and engines in the First World War. Most of the aeroplanes were other companies' designs, but Beardmore did build a few 'home-grown' types.

Times were hard in the 1920s as there were few contracts in austerity peacetime. Beardmore closed their aircraft department, then decided on one last try. They took out a licence from the German Rohrbach company to use their pioneering stressed-skin construction (essentially the standard method today). The strangely-named Inflexible was a jumbo of its day – the 157ft (49m) span (more than a Boeing 707's) made this great trimotor monoplane the largest aircraft in the world when it flew in 1928.

The Inflexible flew well enough and it is a pity this bold venture was not developed into a practical transport, for it was ahead of its time. Beardmore called it a day and this time closed its aircraft division for ever.

Beech 18
classic light twin built for 32 years

Walter Beech specialised in private and business aeroplanes, starting with his Model 17, a smart biplane generally known as the 'Staggerwing' as the top wing was mounted further back than the lower, and first flown in 1932.

The Model 18 twin first flew in 1937. Over 9,000 were to be made and it has been said that over 90% of wartime American navigators and bomb-aimers trained on the type. For a long time the 32 year production run was the longest for any aeroplane.

Beech have continued with quality light aircraft and small airliners, including the 1946 Bonanza with its distinctive 'Vee' tail, some 10,000 of which were made.

Bell 47
first American civil helicopter

One of the most successful helicopters ever made, the little Bell 47 first flew in 1947. Easily recognised by its 'goldfish bowl' glazed nose, nearly 6,000 were made in four countries over a span of 30 years.

Bell HU-1
'Huey' – most widely used helicopter

The first American turbine-powered helicopter, the Bell 204 in civil form or HU-1 (hence the popular 'Huey') in military guise was built in greater numbers than any other helicopter – over 11,000.

The bulk were used in Vietnam for transport, casualty evacuation, and as Hueycobra 'gunships', pioneering the use of armed helicopters now regarded as vital on any battlefield.

Bell P-39 Airacobra
innovative mid-engine fighter

Always willing to be the first to try a new idea, the company founder Larry Bell was one of the first to use a tricycle undercarriage in his 1939 Airacobra, and to make it even more unusual mounted the Allison engine behind the pilot. Putting the weight at the centre of gravity gave good manoeuvrability.

Some might have worried about failure of the fast-spinning propeller shaft between the pilot's legs ruining his marriage prospects in the event of failure but this feature actually gave little trouble. The RAF ordered a batch but found its performance too low for use in Europe.

Most of the 9,584 built were supplied to Russia, as was the case with a similar but improved fighter, the Kingcobra. The Bell fighters were handicapped by a poor engine.

Bell P-59 Airacomet
first American jet

As part of the Allied war effort, Frank Whittle's jet engine technology was passed to America in 1941. Bell did well to fly their Airacomet with two General Electric J31 engines on 1st October, 1942, five months before the Meteor in Britain.

In a sense this was the first jet fighter anywhere, for it was the first jet to fly with guns fitted. Despite the promising start, performance was disappointing and only 64 were built.

KEEPING THE SECRET

Early work on jets was carried out in great secrecy. When the Airacomet was moved on the airfield before its first flight, to disguise its true nature, it was fitted with a dummy propeller.

To give VIPs the chance to experience the then novelty of jet flight, one Airacomet was fitted with a second seat in the nose, but there was a catch – it was an open cockpit!

Bell X-1
first to fly faster than sound

Yet another instance of Bell being the leader, the X-1 (or XS-1 as it was initially) was one of the greatest leaps into the unknown in the history of flight. In the early 1940s there was much talk of a dreaded 'sound barrier' which many believed could never be breached. A handful of very brave men were determined to prove otherwise.

The X-1 was rocket-powered and was launched from a B-29 bomber. The man of destiny was

Bell X-1, First to fly faster than sound

Captain 'Chuck' Yeager who passed the magic Mach 1 on 14th October, 1947.

Improved versions of the straight-wing X-1 reached Mach 2.5 and a swept-wing successor, the X-2, exceeded Mach 3. However the risks were high and there were fatalities. Bell continued with pioneering research aeroplanes, including jet vertical take-off and, another world 'first', the X-5 swing-wing aircraft.

Benoist XIV
world's first passenger aeroplane service

Tom Benoist started the first airline service by aeroplanes (airship services had already operated in Germany) on 21st January 1914 between St. Petersburg, Florida, and Tampa. The distance was 22 miles (35 km).

The Benoist flying-boat could carry just one passenger so it is not surprising that it was unprofitable and the service lasted just a few months. 62 years to the day after Tom Benoist launched his first airline flight, the first fare-paying supersonic travellers embarked on Concorde, vividly illustrating the incredible pace at which airline travel has developed.

Blackburn (later British Aerospace) Buccaneer
low-level strike aircraft

Robert Blackburn started building aeroplanes as early as 1909, and a 1912 Blackburn monoplane is the oldest airworthy British aircraft. Blackburn specialised in naval aircraft, including some fine flying-boats. Sadly, their principal designs at the beginning of World War Two proved inadequate (although a Blackburn Skua pilot won the first Fleet Air Arm victory of the war) and the firm concentrated on building other companies' products.

The Buccaneer was designed specifically for high-speed low-level work. A strike aeroplane may escape radar detection by coming in low, but the penalty is that the airframe must be particularly strong to cope with turbulence at high speeds and low levels.

Designed for carrier use, the Buccaneer originally had two de Havilland Gyron Junior engines and 'blown' wings and tail. This last is a system which produces extra lift by blowing air taken from the engine through slots in the wings. It cut landing speeds by 15 knots, a valuable benefit for landing on a carrier. First flight was in 1958 and service flying started in 1961.

This version was underpowered, decidedly so in the event of one engine failing. The S.2, with two Rolls-Royce Speys, followed in 1965, and made a far better aeroplane. In 1970 the RAF started flying the Buccaneer, and took over the Royal Navy's aircraft when a political decision led to the end of carriers apart from those supporting Harriers. The one other customer was South Africa who took 16, fitted with two rockets for extra take-off power.

Where the 'Brick' excelled was in its smooth ride at low level, where it out-performed many much later types. Buccaneers were finally retired in 1994, having made a brief appearance in the1991 Gulf War.

THE PRICE OF POLITICS

Selection of the Buccaneer for the RAF followed a remarkable saga of political misjudgements. The planned RAF strike aircraft was the TSR2, cancelled by the government in 1964. Instead the government ordered American F-111s – they would be cheaper, wouldn't they? They weren't, and in due course these too were cancelled. Finally, the Buccaneer was ordered to fill the gap, which it did with distinction for 24 years.

Blériot XI
first aeroplane across the English Channel

As the number implies, Blériot had already made 10 aeroplanes before he made his mark on history. He had crashed almost all of them. On 25th July, 1909 he was ready to bid for a £10,000 prize offered by the *Daily Mail* for the first aeroplane flight between France and Britain (it had been done by balloon several times). He had a competitor, Hubert Latham, who was ready for a second attempt after his Antoinette had suffered engine failure over the Channel six days earlier. Blériot forestalled Latham by taking off at 4.41 am. His rival had also planned an early start but the person charged with waking him failed to do so. 36 minutes later Blçriot coaxed his underpowered little monoplane with its 23hp Anzani engine through a gap in the cliffs and landed, rather heavily, near Dover Castle.

Blohm and Voss Bv141
amazing asymetry

The German shipbuilding firm (still a going concern) made a range of fine flying-boats, but the Bv141 was one of the strangest aeroplanes ever made, being totally unsymmetrical. Designed for observation duties, the fuselage and tail were offset to one side of the centre-line. On the other side was a manned nacelle for the 3 crew. The purpose of the bizarre design was to provide the best possible view. Even the tailplane was unsymetrical. Surprisingly enough, when flown in 1938, it handled remarkably well, but perhaps understandably the German Air Ministry balked at such a radical layout and it was not made in quantity.

Boeing 247
trendsetter in airliner design

Boeing 247 – Set the pattern in metal monoplanes

This all-metal monoplane with retractable undercarriage and variable-pitch propellers set the pattern of airliner design until the jet age. Boeing are today linked with large aeroplanes, but until the 247 they had concentrated on small single-engine 'pursuits' (the American term for fighters at the time), including the first American monoplane fighter, the P-26, often called the 'Peashooter'. The 10-passenger 247 flew in February 1933. Its structure owed something to German Rohrbach designs of the 1920s. The 247 started to sell well but Boeing then made a blunder – at the time they owned United Airlines and insisted on completing their order before delivering to anyone else. Other airlines turned to Douglas and the resulting DC-2s and DC-3s swept the 247 from the skies. 75 had been built.

Boeing 707

first American jet airliner

Boeing started studying jet transports as early as 1950. After the 247 they had never rivalled Douglas and Lockheed as airliner builders. Their 1938 Boeing 307 Stratoliner, based on the B-17 bomber, trod new ground in being pressurised, but only 10 were built.

The next dabble in airliners, the double-deck Stratocruiser of 1947, was popular with passengers but only 55 went into airline service. However 888 military transport or tanker versions were made, and this gave Boeing the key to launching what became the 707.

The prototype, then known as the 367-80, flew on 15th July, 1954. Some smiled when the undercarriage collapsed before the first flight, but they were not to smile for long.

At the time, the aircraft was seen mainly as a military transport and tanker. This was astute, for some 800 of these C-135 (transports) and KC-135 (tankers) were to be built, underwriting the enormous financial risk and allowing the civil 707 to be launched. Pan American started transatlantic services in October 1958, just after BOAC with their Comet 4s.

Neither aircraft had true transatlantic range but Boeing soon rose to that challenge with the enlarged 707-320 Intercontinental, establishing the company as the world leader in jet airliners which it has remained ever since.

Engine design, too, was improving fast, helping Boeing in improving the 707 range. Early Pratt & Whitney JT3 engines were replaced by the JT4, then Rolls-Royce offered their Conway 'by- pass' engine, forerunner of the turbofan. 5 airlines chose this engine but Pratt and Whitney went one better by hanging a large 'fan' section on their engine to make the JT3D. The economical, and quieter, turbofan had arrived.

The 707 reigned supreme on long-haul air routes for 12 years. 808 of the airliners were built up till 1980. A shorter-range version, the 720 was offered at one stage. The 707 family ended with the early-warning 'AWACS' aircraft with large radar dishes on the roof. The final examples were 7 for the RAF, completed in 1992.

STRONG AND SAFE

Boeing benefitted from the lessons of the Comet structural failures by using much thicker skin material and 'fail-safe' construction. This is a feature of design which prevents cracks spreading and becoming dangerous.

Test pilot 'Tex' Johnston demonstrated the strength of the 707 by rolling the prototype in public! This was a tricky undertaking on such an aircraft – a German crew tried it on a training flight but ripped the engines off and crashed.

Boeing 727 to 777 (excluding 747 – see below)

best-selling twin and trijet airliners

First flown in 1963, the 727 trijet followed the pattern set by the Caravelle and Trident in mounting the engines at the rear to give an aerodynamically 'clean' wing. So similar did the 727 look to the Trident that there were accusations of copying!

Boeing wasted little time in putting the 727 into service, doing so within a year of the maiden flight. The Trident started test flying a year before the 727 but still entered service later. Early versions seated 130, later expanded to 189. All used Pratt & Whitney JT8D engines.

The 727 made aviation history by becoming the first jet airliner to exceed 1,000 sales.

The smaller 737 followed in 1967. Many questioned whether it would sell against the then well-established BAC 1-11 and Douglas DC-9, but as usual Boeing had judged the market well – some 3,000 have been sold by 1995, the most successful jet airliner ever!

Boeing 737 –
The top selling Jet Airliiner

An astute move was using the same cabin width as the larger airliners, allowing economical six-abreast seating. For the 737, Boeing reverted to under-wing engines and made such play about the advantages of this position (doubtless because the competitors used rear engines) that some 727 customers asked Boeing to desist!

Until the early 1980s the standard engine was the Pratt & Whitney JT8D, but since 1984 developed versions with the more efficient French-American CFM56 have appeared.

The 757, first flown in 1982, is a single-aisle airliner taking between 175 and 250 passengers, broadly replacing the 727. Engines are two Rolls-Royce RB211-535s or Pratt & Whitney 2037/2040s, the former having proved the majority choice, and with good reason, for it has become one of the most reliable engines ever made. Indeed these airliners are now permitted to fly long overwater routes formerly forbidden for twin-engine types.

The 767 is a larger, twin-aisle airliner, first flown in 1981. Choice of engine is between Pratt & Whitney 4052 or General Electric CF6-80. The latest member of the family (in 1996) is, as might be guessed, the 777, first flown in 1994. Boeing looked at enlarging the 767 but opted for an entirely new design with engines from all the big three suppliers on offer.

> An innovation on an airliner is the ability of the outer wing on the Boeing 777 to fold upwards to ease parking at airports, and yes, there is a lock to prevent it folding in the air!

Like every one of the Boeing jetliners, the 777 looks like being a winner, but times are tougher now. Will the upstart Airbus dislodge the mighty Boeing from its perch as the world leader in jet airliners?

Boeing 747
the Jumbo jet

Boeing looked at enlarging the 707 and options such as double-decker layouts before settling on the then revolutionary idea of the 'wide-body' fuselage with twin aisles. More passenger space was squeezed in by extending the cabin to the nose and placing the cockpit above, giving the 747 its characteristic 'hump'. Cynics suggested the hump was to give pilots room to sit on their wallets!

Boeing took enormous financial risk in launching the programme. Everything was planned on a grand scale, including building a brand-new 780 acre factory just for the 747. The new airliner became dubbed the 'Jumbo Jet', and the name stuck. Inevitably there were problems, but the first flight by Jack Waddell on 9th February 1969 was within a couple of months of the original, very tight schedule.

Services were delayed a little due to a problem with the 40,000lb thrust Pratt & Whitney JT9D engines, but even so Pan American were carrying passengers by January 1970, less than a year after first flight. By contrast Concorde flew a month after the 747 but entered service in January 1976.

The 747 soon demonstrated economics about 30% better than the 707s and Douglas DC-8s it replaced. Before long the 747 was virtually alone on the long-haul routes of the world. Now the 747 has been in service for 25 years, but today's models are vastly different from the early examples, giving seat-mile costs some 25% lower. Better engines have played their part, not only from Pratt & Whitney but also from General Electric and Rolls-Royce, whose RB211 has become a popular choice.

Specialised versions have been added for freight, the 'Special Performance' shortened fuselage long range variant (delivery flights of over 10,000 miles (16,000 km) have been flown), and high-density models seating up to 600 passengers.

Boeing's great airliner remains in a class of its own. It has an excellent safety record, although sadly not immune to the scourge of terrorism. It is one of the most successful airliners ever built, with over 1,200 sold and showing every sign of being built for many years to come. Another 25 perhaps?

THE AIRLINERS WHICH CHANGED THE WORLD

The Boeing 747 and the 707 before it are not only formidable technical achievements, they have had an enormous social impact on the world.

Their economic performance has enabled long-haul air fares to plummet in real terms. With long-distance air travel costing less per mile than trains, air tickets have become the bargain of our time, outside Europe anyway.

Millions now visit relatives in distant lands in a way which would have been impossible 40 years ago, and exotic tourist destinations which not long ago were unthinkable for most families are now commonplace (whether that is always good for such places is another matter).

There may be an even more profound benefit too. As so many millions more now travel, could it be that people of different countries might understand each other better, reducing the risk of major wars?

The more hours a day an airliner flies, the more it earns. A 747 might fly 12 to 14 hours per day. It is vital to spend as little time as possible on the 'turn-round' between flights. Before the 747 entered service, one item looked as though it would take longer than anything else on the ground – emptying the ashtrays!

Boeing B-17 Flying Fortress

classic American heavy bomber

The B-17 was to become the most famous of American bombers, although made in much smaller numbers than the later Liberator. The B-17 first flew in July 1935 (as the Boeing 299). It was named 'Flying Fortress', although this was inapt since at that time defensive armament was woefully inadequate. Three months later the prototype crashed killing several crew members – the control locks to prevent wind damage on the ground had not been removed.

The RAF took an early batch in 1941 but losses in daylight bombing were disastrous. The lesson was learned and new versions with more protective guns appeared. American operations started in 1942 and for a time the typically 13 defensive guns kept losses within tolerable levels. By 1943 losses were creeping up as German defences improved and were nearing unbearable levels when salvation arrived in the form of the long-range Mustang escort fighter.

The B-17s were strong and some came home with complete fins or tailplanes on one side missing. A few logged over 100 missions, with a record of 157. 12,731 Flying Fortresses were built. Engines were Wright R-1820 Cyclones of around 1,200 hp.

FIGHTER FORTRESS

A wartime cartoon, referring to the great fire-power of later B-17s, showed a B-17 without bombs shooting enemy aircraft out of the sky, while single-engine fighter-bombers were dropping the bombs.

The cartoonist was nearer reality than he knew! Some B-17s with even more guns but no bombs were sent as escorts. The trial ended when it was found these heavily armed machines could not keep up with the by then lightened bombers on the way home.

B-29 Superfortress

first and, it is to be hoped, only aeroplane to drop nuclear bombs in war

The B-29 was far larger than the B-17 and broke new ground in using pressurised crew compartments and remote controlled gun turrets.

First flight was in 1942 and operations started in 1944. At first, missions were mounted against Japan from India. Losses were heavy due to the long haul over hostile territory and the crossing of the Himalayas. As more Pacific islands were taken by the Americans, raids were mounted over shorter ranges and losses dropped.

The Second World War was brought to an end with the two atomic bombs. On 6th August 1945 Colonel Paul Tibbetts flew B-29 'Enola Gay' to the attack on Hiroshima, followed three days later by Major Sweeney flying 'Bock's Car' to Nagasaki.

The loss of life was enormous but many hundreds of thousands of servicemen were eternally thankful they were spared the ordeal of an assault on Japan, and many Allied prisoners would not have survived much longer the dreadful cruelty inflicted by the Japanese.

B-29s were in action again in Korea, and the RAF flew the type between 1950 and 1955, calling it the Washington. An improved version, the B-50 entered service in 1948 with more powerful engines – 3,500hp Pratt & Whitney Double Wasps. One, 'Lucky Lady II', was the first aeroplane to fly non-stop round the world, with in-flight refuelling.

The mission was originally intended to be a round-the-world flight of three aircraft, with intermediate landings, to demonstrate the long reach of American air power to the Soviet Union. The plan went awry when one aircraft crashed, leaving the Russians unimpressed.

The head of Strategic Air Command, General Curtis LeMay, ordered the Lucky Lady II to start again alone, but this time non-stop. The successful flight, in 1949, took 93 hours.

Boeing B-47 Stratojet
futuristic swept-wing bomber

Sensational in its day, the six-engine B-47 took to the air on 17th December, 1947. Its 35 deg. swept wing and underwing engine pods were radical for the time but set the pattern for large jets to come.

Not only was the B-47 a bold undertaking technically, but it was also a huge production task, for over 2,000 were built, reflecting the importance attached to this bomber in keeping international peace.

Many top military officers and politicians believe it was the presence of the B-47, more than any other factor, which prevented war between East and West at the time.

Boeing B-52 Stratofortress
backbone of American air power for 40 years

Somewhat similar in layout to the B-47, the B-52 was much larger and a totally new design. The eight Pratt & Whitney J57 engines were hung in podded pairs under and forward of the wings. First flown in 1952, the B-52 entered service in 1955. No one at the time would have expected them to be still going strong 40 years later! 744 of the mighty bombers were built, and at the time of writing 148 remain in service, re-engined with TF33 turbofans.

The B-52 is a truly intercontinental bomber. Its capability was shown in 1957 when three flew non-stop round the world, with three in-flight refuellings, in 45 hours. The bomber was used extensively in Vietnam, sometimes controversially, and again in the 1991 Gulf War.

The current B-52H version is being refitted with modern electronics and missiles. It looks as though these mighty old warhorses will be flying for some years yet.

Boeing Vertol CH-47 Chinook
principal heavy transport helicopter of the West

One of the most important transport helicopters ever built, the Chinook had its origins in a series of twin-rotor machines made by the Piasecki company and popularly called the 'Flying Bananas' because of their kinked fuselages. Piasecki became Vertol in 1956 and Boeing-Vertol in 1960.

The Chinook first flew in 1961. The two rotors, which turn in opposite directions, are driven by Textron Lycoming T55 turbine engines of about 5,000 hp in the latest versions. Thanks largely to increases in engine power, present versions carry around 13 tons of cargo, more than the gross weight of early examples!

Most Chinooks have been bought for military use but some are used for civil transports and for oil exploration work. The helicopter has now been in production for 33 years and looks set for many more years of sales yet.

Boeing-Vertol Chinook

For passenger carrying about 18 seats are normally fitted, but to show what it can do when it really tries one carried 147 people on a refugee evacuation!

Boulton Paul Defiant
the flawed fighter

The old-established engineering company Boulton and Paul formed an aircraft division in 1915. Some good designs were made but rarely achieved the success they deserved. In 1934 their Overstrand bomber made its mark on aviation history in being the first with an enclosed, power-operated gun turret.

The company's gun turrets were fitted to many British wartime bombers, and possibly this interest may have clouded their judgement when they conceived the Defiant. The Defiant, with its single Merlin engine, looked right up to date when it first flew in August 1937. However there was a fatal weakness – all the guns were mounted in a turret manned by a second crew member. There were no forward firing guns. The layout had worked in the First World War, but times had changed.

When the first squadron of Defiants appeared in May 1940, German fighters swooped from abeam and suffered heavy losses from those four-gun turrets, but it was to be the only moment of glory for the Defiant. German pilots soon exploited its weakness and losses became so heavy that the Defiants were withdrawn in August.

To make matters worse, baling out of the gunner's position was far from easy. Defiants were switched to nightfighting and achieved some successes until 1942. Most ended their days towing targets.

Breguet 19
possibly largest sales of any inter-war aircraft

Louis Breguet started flying experiments with helicopters in 1907, and just lifted off the ground but without any means of control. He soon realised that the problems of controlling a helicopter were beyond the technology of the day and turned to fixed-wing aeroplanes.

Around 8,450 of his wartime single-engine Breguet 14 bombers and reconnaissance types were made. Its successor, the Breguet 19 appeared in 1921. Some 3,280 were built over the next 12 years in 7 countries.

Many record-breaking flights were made, including a round-the-world flight in 1927-28, a distance record of 4,912 miles (7905 km) in 1929 and the first flight from France to America. These last two were by the French pilots Costes and Bellonte in 'Point d'Interrogation' ('Question Mark'), the most famous of all Breguet 19s.

Breguet Atlantic
pioneer of international collaboration

Nowadays it is common practice to spread the huge cost of advanced aircraft by several countries agreeing to build and buy the same type. The Atlantic anti-submarine aircraft was the first such major project.

Companies in France, Germany, Holland and Belgium took part. Likewise four countries were involved in making the Rolls-Royce Tyne turboprops. Would the parts all fit? They did, and the first Atlantic flew in 1961.

87 Atlantics were built up till 1974. That seemed to be the end, but in 1981 an improved version flew with new electronics and weapon loads. Production restarted in 1989 and is due to continue until 2001, an impressive 40-year run.

By the time the modernised Atlantic flew, Breguet had become part of Dassault. It is typical of that fiercely nationalistic company that dreaded Anglicised words be avoided: Atlantic has become Atlantique!

Brewster F2A Buffalo
America's flawed fighter

If the Boulton Paul Defiant was Britain's dud, the Buffalo was America's! First flown in 1938 as a carrier fighter, it proved nowhere near robust enough for carrier landings. The RAF took delivery of some originally destined for Belgium, but soon rejected them for European use and sent them to the Far East.

When Japan entered the war heavy losses were sustained by all nations flying the Buffalo – it was too slow, lightly armed, and unreliable. Courageous pilots did their best against hopeless odds.

Despite the Buffalo's generally poor showing in combat, there was one theatre of operations where it actually distinguished itself – in Finland.

A batch had been supplied in 1940 and when Russia attacked in the following year a group of experienced and determined pilots showed what they could do even in the Buffalo. They shot down 477 enemy aircraft. 12 pilots accounted for 10 or more each and one was credited with 38.

Perhaps the Buffalo had its redeeming points after all.

Bristol Blenheim and Beaufighter

the famous Bristol twins

In 1934 Frank Barnwell designed a fast twin-engine metal monoplane, the Type 142. Lord Rothermere of the *Daily Mail* bought the aeroplane to jolt officialdom into promoting more advanced British aircraft. When it flew in April 1935 it proved 50 mph (80 kph) faster than the best RAF fighters.

Lord Rothermere called it 'Britain First' and presented it to the nation. His 'stirring' had the desired effect and a bomber version, the Blenheim, flew on 25th June, 1936, entering service in the following year.

All British-built Blenheims used two Bristol Mercury engines, but Canadian-built examples, named Bolingbroke, generally took American engines. Alas, such was the rate of progress at the time that the advanced machine of 1936 was already dated by 1940. By then slow and lightly armed, gallant crews suffered dreadful losses.

Three VCs were among Awards to Gallant Blemheim Crews

In one attack five out of six Blenheims were lost. The feelings and fears of crews preparing for subsequent missions can only be imagined, and regrettably their fears were all too justified, for on another raid only one out of 12 returned. To make matters worse, it was difficult to avoid being shredded by the propellers on baling out. Three V.C.s were awarded to Blenheim pilots.

To be fair to the Blenheim, much of the trouble arose from misguided tactics in sending these bombers in daylight without escorts.

Some Blenheims were adapted as fighters, and at night achieved some success; the first successful radar-assisted night attack in history was recorded on 22nd July, 1940. The Beaufort was a torpedo bomber derived from the Blenheim. It first flew in 1938 and was widely used by the RAF and Royal Australian Air Force. Beauforts gave reasonable service but were plagued by their troublesome Bristol Taurus engines. Some versions used Pratt & Whitney engines to overcome this drawback.

An outstanding action by a Beaufort crew was an attack on the cruiser *Gneisenau* which caused major damage but at the cost of their lives. The pilot, Flying Officer Campbell, was awarded a posthumous VC.

By far the best of the Bristol twins was the Beaufighter. The idea of a twin-engine fighter arose from the urgent need for cannon armament (i.e. firing explosive shells).

At the time it was thought designers would be unable to mount these in the wings of Hurricanes and Spitfires, although later they did just that. Originally dubbed the 'Beau Fighter', the new aeroplane first flew on 20th July, 1939. The unofficial name became adopted as Beaufighter.

With two Bristol Hercules, or in one version Rolls-Royce Merlins, the powerful fighter had a speed of some 320 mph, and with ten forward-firing guns made short work of any enemy who strayed in its way.

The Beaufighter became highly versatile, being used for night-fighting, torpedo-bombing, and ground attack. The low noise level led to the Japanese calling it 'whispering death'. 5,928 Beaufighters were built in Britain and Australia.

THE TRIALS OF RESTORERS

Not one of the 6,458 Blenheims built was preserved in Britain. By the 1970s a group felt strongly that a Blenheim should be rebuilt to honour the brave crews who died in them.

For 12 years they laboured in spare time using derelict parts of abandoned airframes. In 1987 came triumph and once again a Blenheim was seen in the air, but the pleasure was short-lived, for a month later it was damaged beyond repair.

Many would have given up, but those determined men and women worked anew for a further 5 years, until once more a Blenheim can be seen at displays.

A run of mysterious fatal crashes involving Australian-built Beauforts shows the importance and complexity of accident investigation. No defects were ever found in the wreckage.

It was a pathologist who solved the mystery: the cabin heating had been blanked off for Australian use, but the blanks were not gas-tight. Crews had succumbed to carbon monoxide.

Test pilot Bill Pegg force-landed his Beaufighter on a golf course.
He emerged straight in front of the startled managing director's wife, who was playing an adjacent hole.

Bristol Britannia

the fine airliner which was just too late

Bristol saw a need to reduce dependence on military work as the Second World War neared its end. Their first attempt was certainly ambitious, the colossal 8-engine Brabazon. The mighty machine flew in 1949 and crowds looked upwards in wonder as it passed sedately overhead. Less impressed were residents of a village demolished to lengthen the runway at Bristol's airfield.

Nor were airlines too enthusiastic. The Brabazon could carry 100 passengers with 8 large engines when American airliners soon to come would do the same on four. The Brabazon was doomed.

A far better proposition was the Britannia, originally conceived around piston engines but at an early stage redesigned to take four Bristol Proteus turboprops.

The first Britannia flew in August 1952. A second followed late the following year, but in February 1954 pilot Bill Pegg had to make an emergency landing in the Severn Estuary after an engine fire. Various delays followed including engine icing problems and not till February 1957 did this beautiful airliner enter service.

A long-range transatlantic version followed at the end of the year, but as BOAC's Chief Engineer aptly put it "the hounds of the big jets were baying in our traces". Within a year passengers would scorn long-haul airliners with propellers. Just 85 Britannias were made. It was so nearly a success. Three times it was poised for American airline orders, but in the end the delays were crippling – it was just too late.

The Britannia story did not quite end there. In Canada the Canadair company built an anti-submarine version with piston engines called Argus, and a long-range freighter with Rolls-Royce Tyne engines and a swinging tail to ease cargo loading, the CL44. Even that was not quite the last link with the Britannia. The Short Belfast freighter used Britannia wings and tail!

Bristol Bulldog

biplane fighter

The Bulldog single-seat fighter first flew in 1927. It was made from high-tensile steel, giving low maintenance costs. 443 of these fine fighters were built, at one time equipping 10 of the 13 RAF Air Defence squadrons. They were noted for excellent aerobatic handling. A number were supplied to Finland and saw action against Russia in 1939, aquitting themselves well although by then obsolete.

A Bulldog was restored in 1961 but sadly destroyed performing aerobatics at Farnborough in 1964.

> *There was heated argument after the 1964 loss of the Bulldog as to whether historic aeroplanes should be flown. By far the majority feel they should be seen in the air, but should they be subjected to aerobatics?*
>
> *The debate resurfaced in 1993 after a tragic fatal crash of the Rolls-Royce owned Spitfire in similar circumstances.*

Bristol F2A and F2B Fighter

outstanding British Fighter of World War One

Designed by Frank Barnwell, Bristol's designer for 30 years, the F2A flew in September 1916. It was a two-seat biplane with two machine guns, one facing forward and fired by the pilot, the other manned by the gunner. The engine was a 190hp Rolls-Royce Falcon.

First combat experiences early in 1917 were most discouraging as losses were daunting. The problem was one of tactics. They were being flown like the early two-seaters, relying too much on the gunner.

The Fine Bristol Fighter Taught Hard Lessons in Tactics

Once pilots learned to use the forward gun as the primary armament, pointing the aircraft at the enemy, the Bristol Fighter became one of the best of the war.

Most of the 5,308 built were of an improved F2B version. Some other engines were fitted with mixed results as Rolls-Royce were pressed to make enough Falcons. Production started in America, but the end of the war and an unsuitable choice of engine limited output to small numbers.

In Britain, the 'Brisfit' was built until 1927. It remained in RAF service until 1932 while New Zealand kept some veterans flying until 1938. In civilian use a few pioneered the art of 'skywriting' whereby a skilful pilot could release coloured smoke and write an advertising message in the sky.

Bristol Type 170 Freighter
workhorse to the world and car ferry

The 170 was designed as a tough freighter for military use or outback areas. It owed some features to an earlier transport, the 1935 Harrow. A high wing was chosen to ease cargo loading, and for ruggedness the undercarriage was fixed. Engines were two Bristol Hercules.

First flight was in December 1935. Two versions were offered, with and without wide nose doors depending on whether passenger or freight use was planned. Strictly speaking the name Freighter (or more irreverently 'Frightener') applied only to that version (the other was Wayfarer), but the name became widely used for the whole 170 family. 214 were built, so it must be regarded as a success.

It excelled at jobs in remote places which no other aircraft could tackle. On one refugee flight 117 people were lifted. In Britain it was best-known for the cross-channel car ferry services run by Silver City and Air Charter. In the 1950s these were booming so much that many thought the days of sea ferries were numbered, but rising maintenance costs and better ships reversed the balance of power and by the end of the 1960s the air ferries had gone.

In New Zealand trusty Freighters flew a shuttle service across Cook Strait for 35 years, until 1986. For some operators the aircraft were literally irreplaceable. One sold his fleet only to have to buy more later. The last three of these old workhorses ended their flying days in Canada in 1995.

A road-building team in the centre of Australia anxiously awaited the Freighter due with supplies and mail.

To their dismay just a single letter dropped to the mail-starved men – for the leader of the team, his income tax demand.

Bristol 171 Sycamore
first successful British helicopter

Bristol set up a helicopter division in 1945 under Austrian pioneer Raoul Hafner. The Sycamore flew on 27th July, 1947 and became the first British helicopter to be certificated.

178 were built, mostly for military use, including 50 for Germany. A few were used for civil passenger and mail trials, although the Sycamore was too small to be economic. All production machines used single Alvis Leonides engines.

The Sycamore was a success but sadly Bristol never repeated this good start. Many years of testing twin-rotor helicopters led to the meagre reward of 26 Belvederes for the RAF. Bristol Helicopters became part of Westland in 1960.

British Aerospace 146 (now Avro RJ series)
British short-haul airliner

Originally conceived as the Hawker Siddeley 146 in 1973, the 146 did not appear in the air until September 1981. The delay was due to indecision as to whether to launch the airliner. Unusually for a passenger jet, the 146 has a high wing. The four Lycoming ALF502 engines (in present versions Textron Lycoming LF507) are mounted in under-wing pods.

From the start, a major selling point of the 146 has been low noise levels, in some cases allowing services into airports normally closed to jets. The 146 has sold in respectable but not spectacular numbers. 218 were sold before it was relaunched as the RJ series, including some in the tough United States market.

Now British Aerospace have revived an historic name from British aviation in renaming the airliner the Avro RJ (for 'Regional Jet') series.

British Aircraft Corporation One-Eleven
short-haul jet airliner

At one time the BAC One-Eleven looked like being the most successful airliner programme Britain has ever had. At 258 sales it was certainly no failure but it could have done so much better.

The airliner started as a Hunting Percival design before the merger which formed BAC in 1960. With Rolls-Royce Spey engines it was enlarged to become the 74-seat 1-11. The airliner was off to an excellent start in 1961 with an order for 10 from British United followed soon after by an order from the American airline Braniff, an unprecedented mark of confidence in a foreign airliner yet to fly. The large carrier American followed. Far ahead of its nearest competitor, the Douglas DC-9, the airliner looked a real winner.

First flight came in August 1963, but two months later came disaster. The prototype crashed killing all seven on board. A 'deep stall' had occurred in which the high tail had been masked by the wing. BAC were criticised for not having fitted a tail parachute which could have allowed recovery. The lesson was learned and a tail parachute fitted. On a later test the pilot deployed it but forgot to release it, causing a rather public landing in a field.

There was to be yet another mishap before the test programme ended. Now airline managers were wondering: three accidents? Meanwhile the DC-9 was catching up. Not long after airline services began a Braniff aircraft broke up in a thunderstorm and the airline Mohawk also suffered a fatal accident. It did not help. Possibly the airliner could have recovered from all this, but its development was limited by the Spey engine being a little too small. This arose because of a disastrous decision to scale the Trident airliner down, for which the engine was designed. BAC were never able to stretch the airliner in the way Douglas did with the DC-9, which expanded from 90 seats to 180.

One-Elevens did sell throughout the world and have served well, but the thousands of DC-9s and Boeing 737s flying are a pointer to what might have been.

British Aircraft Corporation/Sud Aviation Concorde
(now British)
Aerospace/Aérospatiale)

only successful supersonic airliner

Concorde has been in service so long that it is easy to forget what an enormous technical achievement is involved in flying 100 passengers at twice the speed of sound at costs at least approaching economic levels.

The British and French governments signed an agreement in 1962 to build a supersonic airliner. There was no cancellation clause; had there been, there would surely have been no Concorde. The designers aimed to match the economics of the Boeing 707-320. They were not to know that before Concorde would enter service the Boeing 747 would revolutionise long-haul travel, and that matching its predecessor would no longer be enough.

Concorde – 20 Years of Supersonic Service

First flight was on 2nd March, 1969 in the hands of French test pilot André Turcat. World airlines had placed options on 74 Concordes, so there was ground for optimism, but what were those mutterings about rising costs?

Opposition there was, even to the existence of an 'anti-Concorde' group. All sorts of dire events were foreseen: sonic booms would devastate those below, the atmosphere would be damaged, and hapless stewardesses would become infertile from radiation. By all accounts this last at least has proved unfounded!

The task was more complex than originally foreseen. Concorde has many unique and complicated systems, including an array of movable intake doors and ramps, a system to pump fuel between tanks to trim the aircraft in cruise, variable nozzles and reheat for the Bristol Olympus 593 engines.

To provide a good view for the pilot on take-off and landing, the nose hinges down, or 'droops'. When parked at the terminal it is raised again – Concorde looks better that way! All these systems and more needed testing, and it would not be until January 1976 that passenger services would start, six years later than originally planned.

The delays not only saw the Boeing 747 become established, offering an alternative for airline investment, but they greatly increased the cost of Concorde. Finally fuel prices shot up in 1973, hitting Concorde more than subsonic airliners. The options melted away, leaving just the British and French national airlines who were virtually given their Concordes.

Was it all worth while? At a cost of £1,200 million for 14 airliners to enter service, Concorde must be rated a commercial failure, and yet . . . . wherever Concorde flies people look up and point "there's Concorde". The world would have been a duller place (though admittedly a quieter one) if it had never been made.

When the Dutch airline KLM began studying supersonic transports, the name of the leader of the group was Boom.

Incidentally, one oft-quoted 'fact' about Concorde is a fallacy. It does not fly faster than a rifle bullet. Faster than a pistol bullet would be more accurate.

However, it is true that Conc orde travels faster than the sun when flying westbound. Passengers can experience oddities such as the sun rising in the evening.

Air France even offered a special flight at the end of 1976 to enable revellers to celebrate the New Year three times, once in Paris, again over the Atlantic (actually re-entering the old year), and finally in Washington. What were the hangovers like?

Britten-Norman BN-2 Islander (now Pilatus Britten-Norman)
rugged light transport

John Britten and Desmond Norman made crop-spraying equipment. In the 1960s they realised there was no modern utility aircraft to replace the de Havilland Rapide biplane.

Enterprising men as they were, they designed their own. The Islander, which first flew in June 1965, is a rugged 10-seater with a high wing, fixed undercarriage, and two Lycoming piston engines. Clearly they had judged the market well, for some 1,200 have been sold all over the world.

Unfortunately the sales success was not matched financially and the company was sold in 1971, and the new owners in turn were bought by the Swiss firm Pilatus in 1979. Production was moved to Romania with aircraft fitted out at Bembridge, Isle of Wight.

In 1970 an enlarged 17-seat three-engine version was introduced, the Trislander. Ingeniously, the third engine was mounted on the tail fin. Military versions are offered under the name Defender, with the option of Allison 250 turboprops. The Islander family exceeded 10 million flying hours in 1994, a tribute to the foresight of its designers.

Canadair CL215/415
rare modern flying-boats

These Canadian products are a rarity in the 1990s, a series of flying-boats and amphibians still being built. The CL215 flew, with piston engines, in 1967. Its principal function was seen as 'water-bombing', scooping up water from lakes to bomb forest fires, a job hitherto carried out by a selection of World War Two veterans.

The Canadairs have proved popular in parts of the world vulnerable to forest fires, and 125 of the original version were made. The CL415 has turboprop engines and larger water tanks, being able to drop 6 tons per run. A transport amphibian carries 35 passengers.

Canadair Regional Jet
50-seat airliner

Canadair bought the rights to a business jet, the Learstar 600, and sold over 250 as the Challenger. Canadair expanded the Challenger into the Regional Jet airliner, first flown in 1991. About 80 have been sold at the end of 1994.

Caproni-Campini CC2
pioneering Italian 'jet'

Gianni Caproni started making aeroplanes in 1910 and built a range of fine designs. In 1921 he built a colossal airliner, his 100 passenger Ca.60, popularly known as the 'Capronissimo'. Nine wings should have borne the monster aloft, but in the event they never did – it crashed on its maiden flight.

In a sense, the CC2 became the second jet aeroplane in the world to fly, on 28th August, 1940. But was it really a 'jet'? The powerplant designed by Secondo Campini comprised a three-stage fan driven by a 900hp piston engine. It was therefore not a gas turbine, but more accurately a multi-stage propeller in a duct.

However, it did include two pointers to the future in jets, afterburning and a variable nozzle. Maximum speed was a disappointing 230 mph (370 kph), far below that of contemporary fighters.

> *What was the CC1, the first 'jet' design by the partnership?*
> *Similar in layout, it was expected to be supersonic!*
> *In view of the actual performance of the CC2 this hope*
> *must be considered optimistic! It was never built.*

Cessnas

leading builder of private and business aeroplanes

The Cessna company was set up in 1927 and became one of the world's principal suppliers of light aircraft. The Cessna 172, first flown in 1955, became a mainstay of flying schools all over the world. At its peak, production reached 7 a day.

For various reasons including the huge costs of legal claims in the event of accidents (although Cessnas have a good safety record), the company moved away from the part of the market they had dominated and concentrated on business jets and light transports. A whole family of small jets is sold under the name Citation, although the name covers several quite different types.

Now Cessna have changed course again and are re-entering light aircraft building, starting with their old favourite the 172.

Cierva Autogiros

pioneering rotorcraft

The Spaniard Juan de la Cierva turned to rotary-winged flight to avoid the dangers of landings and take-offs in fixed-wing aeroplanes. From 1926 he built a range of autogyros ('Autogiro' was a product name for the Cierva company) with which he achieved some success. Cierva himself was killed in an airliner take-off accident in 1936, an ironic fate for one who had sought to remove just that sort of hazard from flying.

Unlike a helicopter, the blades were not driven by the engine, but were turned by the forward speed of the craft, which had an ordinary propeller. It could not hover, although it could descend almost vertically. It did not need the complex rotor control of a helicopter.

After the war the Cierva company built a mighty three-rotor helicopter, the Air Horse. An odd feature was a large strut right in front of the pilot's eyes. The Air Horse crashed, and Cierva became absorbed into Saunders-Roe.

> *Spinning the rotor up prior to take-off was a comical process on early autogyros. A rope was wound round the rotor shaft and pulled sharply by ground helpers, after which the pilot immediately taxied as fast as possible around the field until the rotor was spinning fast enough to become airborne.*
>
> *Sometimes the process had to be repeated several times before succeeding.*

Cody biplanes
first aeroplane flights in Britain

American-born Samuel Cody flew his British Army Aeroplane Number 1 on 16th October, 1908. Cody developed further biplanes but he was killed whilst flying one of these in 1913.

REMARKABLE SAMUEL CODY

Cody was one of the 'characters' of early aviation. A flamboyant showman, he had made his name by spectacular demonstrations of horsemanship and shooting. He was not, however 'Buffalo Bill' Cody, who lived a little earlier.
Turning from equestrianism to aviation, he made a series of man-lifting kites for army use. They were remarkably stable and safe. From there he moved on to his historic aeroplane flights. He seemed to have an intuitive feel for aerodynamics, for he had no academic background and was unable to read or write.

Consolidated B-24 Liberator
principal American heavy bomber

If asked to name one wartime American bomber, most people would doubtless name the Flying Fortress, yet about half as many again were built of the B-24.

The B-24 was proposed by Consolidated in January 1939 as a more advanced complement to the B-17. In an astonishingly fast timescale, the prototype flew on December 29th of that year.

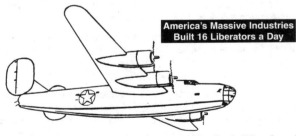

America's Massive Industries Built 16 Liberators a Day

The B-24 used an efficient slender wing, known as the Davis Wing from its originator, and was one of the first with a tricycle undercarriage. The bomber was easily recognised by its wide almost circular twin fins. Engines were four Pratt & Whitney Twin Wasps.

The RAF was an early user, taking advantage of the great range for Atlantic convoy protection and as a ferry aeroplane taking crews to America ready for flying new aircraft eastbound. For similar reasons the USAAF tended to use the B-24 in the Pacific, but it did still participate in some notable raids including dangerous low-level attacks on Romanian oil production at Ploesti.

Early Liberators were criticised for having insufficient forward-facing guns, but once this was put right the aeroplane was well respected. One returned home after being hit by a 500lb bomb from above!

One unusual plan was for some B-24s to be used as flying bombs. The crew were to take off, set the bomber on course for the target, and bale out. On one trial the bomb exploded prematurely, killing Joseph Kennedy Jnr., older brother of the future president.

AMERICA'S INDUSTRIAL MIGHT

The B-24 was a prodigious production programme. 18,432 were built (some sources give over 19,000). No other bomber in history matched these numbers.

Five production lines were set up. One, at Forth Worth, Texas (where else?) is often quoted as the 'mile-long assembly hall'. It wasn't quite, but it was pretty close.

Over 3 years the average output from all plants was around 16 Liberators a day. Some in Japan had warned of the danger of underestimating American industrial output – how right they were!

American bomber squadrons brought to a fine art, literally, decoration of their aircraft.

Highly colourful painted depictions of cartoon figures or whatever took the crew's fancy, embellished the nose, but it will be no surprise to find the favourite subject was well-proportioned, but less-well dressed ladies.

Some of the artwork was most attractive and there are aviation historians who specialise in nose

THE DARING PLOESTI RAIDS

The Ploesti refineries in occupied Romania were a vital source of oil to GErmany. The two raids on these strategic targets were symbolic of the extreme courage shown by so many bomber crews.

In the second attach, in August 1943, 54 of the 179 Liberators failed to return, and 98 more were damaged. 532 men died in this one mission, pressing home their determined low-level attacks.

Consolidated (Convair) B-36
bomber colossus, the 'Mighty Peacemaker'

In 1941 the U.S. government faced the possibilty that Germany might over-run the whole of Europe and conceived the idea of a mighty bomber able to reach Europe and return, a heroic 12,000 mile objective. Because of the huge size of the task and other priorities, first flight was delayed till August 1946.

The great 230ft (71m) span bomber needed 6 Pratt & Whitney Wasp Majors of 3,000 hp (initially), driving 'pusher' propellers to give better airflow over the wing. The engines could be reached by a crawl-way in the wing, and due to the length of the fuselage railed trolleys carried crew members between positions.

Heads turned whenever the awesome machine passed majestically overhead, but it was soon clear the B-36 was underpowered. Adding a few jet engines would do the trick, so two General Electric J47s were hung under each wing, making the propulsion system 'six turning, four burning'. In cruise the jets and some of the piston engines could be shut down when there was little risk.

Some were built for reconnaissance, and to give extra range various schemes were tried for launching small reconnaissance jets from the B-36, and Republic RF-84 'parasites' did enter limited service. A transport version was made, the great double-deck 400-seat XC- 99. Only one was built. 385 B-36s were built up till 1954. They ended their days at the end of the 1950s as Boeing B-52s replaced them.

There was never an official name, but 'the Mighty Peacemaker' was widely used, for many believed the B-36 did indeed deter aggressive intentions from the East.

> *An unusual version of the B-36 was planned, with nuclear power! It was never built, although as research for it one B-36 flew with a nuclear reactor aboard.*

Consolidated PBY Catalina
most successful flying boats ever built

The first version of what became the Catalina flew in 1935 as the XP3Y-1 What a mouthful U.S. Navy numbers were! Designer Isaac 'Mac' Laddon, who was also responsible for the Liberator and Convairliners, produced a parasol wing (mounted on a strut above the fuselage) with the two Pratt & Whitney Wasp engines mounted as close together as propeller clearance permitted. The wing floats swung up in flight to form the wing-tips.

The RAF was an early user, needing its long range to protect convoys. However it was less well armed than the shorter-range Sunderland – you can't have everything! The RAF gave the name Catalina, later also adopted by the U.S. Navy. It was an RAF Catalina which found the battleship Bismark after she had eluded the British fleet, and led to her sinking. Two V.C.s were awarded to Catalina pilots. 196 U-boat sinkings were claimed.

Some 3,281 Catalinas were built including some in Canada, known as Cansos, but excluding a number made under licence in Russia, making it by far the most successful of all flying boats. 1,428 were built as amphibians. Stories persisted of these being landed on water with wheels down or with them raised on land, some at least no doubt apocryphal.

Post-war some record long-distance flights were made with Catalinas. Many were used as airliners, and possibly the world's last scheduled flying-boat services were flown in Chile until 1983. A few remain in service as water-bombers, and these 50-year-old veterans may continue in this role for a few years yet.

> *American Catalina crews had an unusual weapon to make Japanese ground gunners 'keep their heads down' – beer bottles!*
>
> *When dropped (empty needless to say) they made a whistling sound similar to that of real bombs.*

ConvairLiners
early post-war airliners

Convair were one of many companies seeking to build a 'Douglas DC-3 replacement'. Their first bid was a twin-engine 30-seater, the Convair 110 which flew in 1946. Airlines advised Convair to enlarge it and add pressurisation. As the 240 it flew in March 1947, already backed by an order from American Airlines for 100. This airline called them ConvairLiners and the name became widely used. Engines were two Pratt & Whitney Wasp Majors.

The airliner was excellent but a long strike and underpricing led to financial problems and a change of ownership for Convair. The 340 was an improved and enlarged 44-seat version, while the 440 had better soundproofing and detail refinements. Altogether 1,076 ConvairLiners were built, many as military transports.

In later years it was hit by the lure of the turbine power of the Viscount, but this suggested a way of extending the lives of the Convairs – why not convert them to turboprops? First to enter the race, and alas the first to fall, was Napier with their Eland engine. Some had entered service before Napier's owners saw daunting costs ahead and ended the programme. The most successful conversion used the Allison 501 engine. The aircraft was renumbered Convair 580. Lastly, Convair themselves offered the Rolls-Royce Dart, resultant conversions being numbered 600 and 640, but to provide enough power a little too much was expected of that fine engine and reliability was less than in other airliners.

One airline president called the Convairs 'the best airframes ever made'. The fact that nearly 100 were still in service in 1995 and that at least one has exceeded 140,000 landings, believed to be the record for any aeroplane, certainly makes it an excellent candidate.

Convair 880 and 990

ill-fated medium range jet airliners

Convair entered the jet airliner business later than Boeing or Douglas. The 880 was designed to a TWA requirement, but started with an unfortunate decision to make the cabin 5-abreast, compared with 6-abreast of the competitors. The economic disadvantage so caused was virtually impossible to remedy.

First flight was in January 1959, and services started with Delta in 1960. Engines were 4 General Electric CJ-805 turbojets. Just 65 were built, despite Convair's promotion as the fastest airliner in the world. Most were withdrawn by the mid 1970s. The 990 was an improved version featuring an 'aft-fan' version of the CJ-805 to give better economy.

Serious drag problems emerged and airline interest waned. Only 37 were sold. At the time the 880 and 990 programme was quoted as being responsible for the largest financial loss on any one product in business history.

WHAT'S IN A NAME?

The 880 went through a bewildering series of names. It started as the 'Model 22 Skylark 600' – the last number referred to the speed in mph. It then became the 'Golden Arrow', thanks to a gold anodised finish then planned.

When that idea was dropped the name became Convair Jet 880, and finally the 'jet' was dropped to become Convair 880. Why 880? It is 600 mph in feet per second!

Convair B-58 Hustler

first supersonic bomber

First flown in 1956, this four-jet delta bomber had a most impressive performance for its day, being capable of Mach 2 on the power of its General Electric J79 engines. To achieve this, a complex system of variable intakes and nozzles was needed, in some ways pointing the route later followed by Concorde. Unusually, bombs were carried in a long jettisonable pod mounted below the fuselage.

The B-58 set many world records and had outstanding performance. Why then, had the 116 built been withdrawn from service by the end of 1969? It is believed the reasons were a high accident rate and rising maintenance costs.

TRANSPORT OF DELIGHT?

Convair considered a transport version of their B-58, carrying passengers in the under-fuselage pod – with windows but presumably without the pod jettisoning facility.

Convair Deltas
fine fighters after early disappointment

Advised by Alexander Lippisch, who had flown deltas since the 1930s, Convair flew the world's first delta jet on 18th September, 1948, the XF-92A. Convair followed this with an operational fighter, the F-102, intended to reach Mach 1.5. When it flew in 1953 there was dismay – try as they might, it would not even reach Mach 1. Never had such a shortfall in speed happened.

Worries increased when it crashed on its seventh flight. The situation was desperate, for at that time of Cold War tension production had started. To the rescue came an aerodynamicist, Richard Whitcomb, with his 'Area Rule', which suggested that for supersonic aircraft the cross-section should change smoothly from nose to tail. To compensate for the bulge of the wings, add extra bulges on the rear fuselage. It worked, and the F-102 reached its design speed.

After this unpromising start the F-102 served well for 20 years, from 1956. It broke new ground in being the first fighter without guns, relying wholly on missiles. Later combat experience would show this to be a mistake. The F-106 was a developed version with more powerful engine, more advanced electronics and missiles. Convair also tested a water-based Delta, the Sea Dart, flown in 1953. It took off on retractable hydro-skis, and could reach Mach 1 in a shallow dive, thought to be the only marine aeroplane ever to do so. Prototypes only were made.

Curtiss C-46 Commando
rugged transport

First flown in 1940, the twin-engine C-46 became one of the principal Allied transports. Because its use was concentrated in the Far East it never became as familiar in Europe as the ubiquitous C-47/Dakota. 3,182 were built. The type was still in service with the USAF in Vietnam.

Many served with civil freight airlines, mainly in North and South America, for many years, and a few veterans may still be flying.

Curtiss flying-boats
first successful marine aircraft and first across the Atlantic

Glenn Curtiss was one of the earliest pioneers, flying his 'June Bug' in June 1908. On 26th January 1911 his 'Hydroaeroplane' proved to be the first successful water-based aircraft. Shortly afterwards he became the first to fly a flying-boat (with a hull, in contrast to a seaplane which uses floats).

Curtiss flying-boats were widely used in the First World War, including a number by the RNAS who also used the British-built adaptations, the Porte Felixtowes. In November 1918 the flying-boat NC-1 established a world record by carrying 51 people.

The greatest triumph came the following year when three U.S. Navy flying-boats set out to make the first Atlantic crossing by air. Two came down in the sea, but NC-4 flown by Lt. Cdr. Albert Read reached Lisbon, via the Azores, on 28th May 1919.

Curtiss JN 'Jenny'
classic World War One trainer

Curtiss combined two 1914 types, his Models J and N to create the JN, hence 'Jenny'. Over 8,000 were to be built, and almost every American pilot of the First World War was trained on a Jenny. Usual engine was a Curtiss OX-5.

In postwar years many of the 'barnstorming' pilots used Jennies, including Charles Lindbergh of transatlantic flight fame.

Curtiss P-40 Warhawk
World War Two fighter

Curtiss had designed a range of fine fighters or 'pursuits' throughout the 1920s and 1930s including their long-lasting P-6 Hawk biplane fighters. The P-40 flew in October 1938. Essentially it was an earlier radial-engine fighter, the P-36, refitted with a liquid-cooled Allison engine. Some later versions used Packard-built Rolls-Royce Merlins.

Over 15,000 Warhawks were built, many for the RAF who used the names Tomahawk and Kittyhawk. The RAF considered its performance insufficient for use in Europe, but it was widely used in the Middle and Far East. It was considered a good fighter but not in the Spitfire or Mustang class.

The great Curtiss company never made the transition to the jet age and faded away after the war.

Dassault Falcon series
business jets

Dassault, then mainly a military aircraft builder, was one of the first to enter the business jet market. The first version, flown in 1963, was called the Mystère 20, but astutely Dassault arranged to sell it in America via Pan American Airways under the name Falcon, and the company has used this name for marketing ever since.

A highly successful series of Falcons have been built over the last 30 years, including some trijet designs. However, the company's attempt to move into airliner design was a failure – their Mercure was limited to just 10 sales to the French domestic airline Air Inter.

Dassault Mirage
outstanding jet fighters

Dassault was formed by Marcel Bloch, who had produced some successful designs under that name in the 1930s. He refused to collaborate with the Germans and nearly paid for his stand with his life. When he reformed the company after the war he forsook the Bloch name since the company had supplied the Germans, and adapted the code-word used by his brother and himself in the Resistance, Char D`assault (battle-tank).

After the war Dassault built the Ouragan fighter, followed by the swept-wing Mystère, both widely used by the French Air Force. In 1955 Dassault flew the MD550 'Mystère Delta'.

Incredibly, the British government let Dassault test the record-breaking Fairey Delta 2, and based on this knowledge the improved Mirage III was flown in 1956. The engine was a SNECMA Atar. The Mirage III delta became a world-wide success, some 1,400 being built.

The fighters were used with devastating effect by Israel in the 1967 'six-day' war, knocking out most of the Egyptian air force within hours. Paradoxically, France then embargoed any further deliveries to Israel, which that country overcame by making their own versions.

The Mirage 5 had simpler electronics, and was originally intended for Israel. Although never delivered to that country, a number of others preferred this simpler version. The Mirage IV was a nuclear bomber, similar in layout to a much larger Mirage III.

Dassault dabbled with vertical take-off Mirages. First they built a research aeroplane, the Balzac, with a battery of Rolls-Royce lift jets and a single propulsion engine. It performed impressively but set the grisly record of crashing twice with fatal results, having been rebuilt after the first accident.

The Balzac was followed by the Mirage IIIV fighter, which reached Mach 2.4 in 1966, the highest speed ever reached by a vertical take-off aircraft. Despite this, the programme was cancelled later the same year because of the huge costs.

Dassault kept the name Mirage for the totally different F1, which abandoned the delta for a thin swept wing, giving better low-speed handling and a more acceptable ride at low level. It first flew at the end of 1966.

A return was made to the delta with the Mirage 2000 series, first flown in 1978. At first glance it might look like the older Mirage III, but there is a world of difference in the electronics ('fly-by wire' control) coupled with a wing whose camber can be varied to some extent. Manoevrability is incomparably better than the older aeroplane.

Latest of the Dassault combat aircraft is the Rafale, first flown in 1990 and due to enter service in 1997. Like many modern fighters it uses a delta wing with small 'canard' foreplanes. The manoeuvrability of these fighters with modern electronic controls is almost unbelievable.

Israel had already paid for 50 Mirage 5s when the embargo was placed on their delivery.

Not only did the French government refuse to deliver them, they even sent Israel a bill for storage!

de Havilland Comet

first jet airliner

There were actually two Comets made by the company, the first being a pre-war racer which won the 1934 MacRobertson Race to Australia and completed many fine trailblazing flights.

The post-war airliner was a courageous pioneering venture. During the war Britain had built exclusively combat aeroplanes, leaving America to establish a commanding lead in airliners. De Havilland saw the jet airliner as a way of leaping ahead in airliner design. The task was a difficult one, for the early jet engines guzzled fuel. The design which emerged was perhaps the most beautiful of all jet airliners. There were no engine pods, for the four de Havilland Ghost engines were buried in the moderately swept wing.

John Cunningham first flew the Comet on 27th July, 1949. The world's first jet airliner services started on 2nd May 1952. Passengers marvelled at halved flight times, turbine smoothness and the quietness within the cabin. Few realised that the metal between them and the sky outside was about the thickness of a postcard.

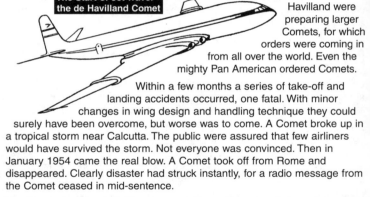

The Start of Jet Travel – the de Havilland Comet

Meanwhile de Havilland were preparing larger Comets, for which orders were coming in from all over the world. Even the mighty Pan American ordered Comets. Within a few months a series of take-off and landing accidents occurred, one fatal. With minor changes in wing design and handling technique they could surely have been overcome, but worse was to come. A Comet broke up in a tropical storm near Calcutta. The public were assured that few airliners would have survived the storm. Not everyone was convinced. Then in January 1954 came the real blow. A Comet took off from Rome and disappeared. Clearly disaster had struck instantly, for a radio message from the Comet ceased in mid-sentence.

The fleet was grounded. After thorough inspections revealed no clues to the disaster, services were resumed. In April another Comet disappeared, also after leaving Rome. This time the Comet 1 was grounded for ever. By an epic of salvage the Royal Navy, helped by Italian vessels, recovered much of the wreckage from the first loss from the sea near Elba.

The parts were reassembled on a framework at Farnborough. Meanwhile a Comet was placed in a great water-tank and water pumped into the fuselage under pressure, then released, to simulate the flight loads of pressurisation. Eventually the fuselage split. The metal skin had failed in fatigue under the stress of pressurisation.

The lessons were applied to the larger Comet 4 with Rolls-Royce Avon engines. These airliners started the first jet transatlantic service on 4th October 1958. A number of airlines bought the Comet 4 series, but effectively de Havilland had lost their lead in jet airliners. The Comet 4 would never be able to match the much larger and longer-range Boeing 707s and Douglas DC-8s.

There was one last chapter in the Comet story. The Hawker Siddeley (by then inheritor of de Havilland designs) Nimrod anti-submarine aircraft, first flown in 1967, was based on Comet wings and tail. An entirely new, deeper fuselage is packed with electronics for its task. Instead of the Rolls-Royce Avon engines of the Comet 4, four of the more economical Rolls-Royce Spey turbofans were fitted. In cruising flight, only two are used. This last link with the Comet remains in service with the RAF.

De Havilland DH125
Britain's most successful business jet

The DH125, briefly marketed as the Jet Dragon, first flew in 1962 and went on to become a highly successful business jet. However, its commercial history is complicated for it has been sold under 5 different company names!

Starting as the DH125 it became Hawker Siddeley 125, British Aerospace 125, Raytheon 800, and Hawker 800, this last being a marketing name used by Raytheon, the American company which bought the rights to the aeroplane from British Aerospace.

Early versions used two Bristol Siddeley (later Rolls-Royce) Viper engines. Later quieter and more efficient American engines were substituted. Over 700 have been sold, about two-thirds in North America. Most have been for company aircraft, but a number have been used as military transports. One early military user bought 4 but flew 3 of them in formation into a mountain.

The future of the programme seems in doubt at the time of writing.

THE RISE OF THE BUSINESS JET

Hundreds of companies now fly their own jet aeroplanes. Many might think these are executive toys or status symbols, but usually they are earning their keep as an efficient way of moving key people. These are not always senior managers: they may be fitters needed for an urgent repair of equipment.

Company aircraft fly to and from airfields which may be far more convenient than major airports, and flights are timed to suit their users. Meetings need not be curtailed to catch a scheduled flight, and business can be continued in the air. Above all, it saves the waste of highly-aid personnel travelling to airports and waiting for flights.

Despite these proven benefits, many companies are still worried that outsiders and shareholders may consider business jets to be frivolous. For this reason, few paint their names on the aircraft.

De Havilland Dove and Heron
light transports

The 8-seat Dove, first flown in 1945, was used all over the world as a light airliner and company aeroplane. Like many de Havilland designs, it was noted for its elegance.

About 540 of this highly successful aeroplane were sold. Engines were two de Havilland Gipsy Queens, although in later years conversions were offered in America with more modern engines.

The Heron was designed on similar lines with four engines and around 17 seats. It became widely used as a feeder-liner. 148 were sold.

De Havilland Dragon and Dragon Rapide
biplane light transports

The Dragon 6-seat transport first flew in 1932 and became a popular light airliner, to the extent of 114 sold by the parent company and 87 built in Australia. A scaled-up 4-engine airliner was produced as the DH86, with elegantly tapered wings. 62 were made.

By far the most successful of the series was the DH89 Rapide, which adopted the tapered wings of its larger cousin giving a pleasing appearance to this biplane. It was widely used as a light airliner before and after the war, including BEA's Highlands services and those to the Isles of Scilly.

The RAF used a version for navigation training and communications which they named Dominie. 685 were made.

WAS HE CARRIED AWAY?

The Dragon was used to open remote parts of Britain to air services. Naturally, passengers were few in number, and must often have been small groups on business or on pleasure trips.

On one particular flight the pilot, who was noted as a practical joker (not known by the passengers, of course), sat in one of the passenger seats in ordinary clothes.

The departure time passed, and the passengers began to wonder what was going to happen.

The pilot sighed, rose, and announced to the passengers: "The pilot hasn't turned up, so I'm going to have a go at flying this thing myself."

He proceeded to the cockpit, leaving alarmed passengers wondering what to do. He then explained that he *was* the pilot.

Relief! It was a highly-successful trip!

de Havilland Mosquito

outstandingly versatile combat aircraft of World War Two

De Havilland proposed the idea of a fast medium bomber relying entirely on its speed for safety.

To avoid compromising performance, it would be unarmed. To make best use of spare skills and avoid scarce materials, it would be made of wood. The company also

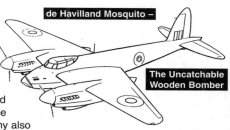

de Havilland Mosquito –

The Uncatchable Wooden Bomber

had experience of building the fast Comet racer and a remarkably 'clean' airliner, the Albatross, using advanced wooden construction methods. Engines were to be two Rolls-Royce Merlins.

There was much official opposition, for the idea of omitting guns was anathema to many diehards, but Sir Wilfrid Freeman of the Air Council became an enthusiast and overcame the sceptics.

First flight was on 25th November 1940 by Geoffrey de Havilland Junior. Here was the world's fastest combat aeroplane. After official indecision as to whether early Mosquitos should be bombers or for reconnaissance, operations started in July 1941 in the latter role. As production increased, versions were developed for bombing and nightfighting, in both duties proving wholly successful.

A 4,000lb bomb could be carried to Berlin (on longer runs a heavier load than a Flying Fortress), and loss rates at around 1% were far below those of any other bomber. Some impressive precision raids were performed. In January 1943 three Mosquitos struck Berlin to coincide with a speech by Goering. In February 1944 a brilliantly executed raid on Amiens jail allowed 258 members of the French resistance to escape, although the strike leader, Percy Pickard, was killed. Three raids on Gestapo buildings in Denmark and Oslo saved many patriots.

7,781 Mosquitos were built. Some 400 firms were involved including many furniture makers, coffin builders and those with similar skills who could handle the wooden construction. The Mosquito was one of the outstanding aeroplanes of the war.

It was dubbed 'The Wooden Wonder' (although there was an alternative 'The Termite's Dream'!), or simply the 'Mossie'. The Hornet was of similar appearance but smaller and in fact a new design. It was the last and fastest RAF piston-engine fighter.

De Havilland Moths

pre-war light aeroplanes for the world

Geoffrey de Havilland had long wished to built a practical light aeroplane for private and club use. The DH60 Moth first flew on 22nd February 1925. The engine was adapted from a war-surplus unit and called the Cirrus. Immediately it became a success and established British private flying on a large scale.

Later, engine designer Frank Halford was urged to design a new engine, which emerged as the Gipsy, first flown in 1928. Gipsy Moths sold all over the world, with production starting in several other countries. Numerous long-distance record flights were made in Moths, all feats of endurance in those open cockpits in all weathers. Other Moths followed. There was the high-wing cabin Puss Moth, holder of many world records, after an early high accident rate due to wing flutter problems.

However, the most famous of all was the DH82 Tiger Moth, first flown in 1931. It became the standard basic trainer for the Commonwealth, and few wartime RAF pilots would not have handled a Tiger in their training days. 7,149 were built, including some in Canada which in deference to local weather had enclosed cockpits. It proved an excellent trainer, being responsive but not too easy to fly.

In desperate days there were even plans to fit bombs to Tiger Moths in case of invasion. Even more bizarre was the 'paraslasher', a knife on a long pole below the Tiger to be flown among descending enemy parachutists and deflate their canopies. It is as well it was not needed.

The RAF kept the Tiger until the early 1950s, when large numbers were sold into civilian hands. It was also widely used for glider towing. Many carefully preserved examples remain airworthy.

> *The passenger in the front seat of a Tiger Moth on a bumpy day felt sick and leaned over the side accordingly.*
>
> *The pilot assumed he must have seen something interesting below and leaned over in the same direction to look .....*

de Havilland (later Hawker Siddeley) Trident

the fatally shrunk airliner

The state airline BEA needed a medium-range jet airliner for European routes. De Havilland responded with the DH121 130-seat trijet. Most regrettably BEA then decided they needed a much smaller aeroplane and it was scaled down to around 100 seats. This proved a fatal mistake, for not only was much time lost in the redesign but for other airlines the new version was too small.

First flight was in January 1962, and services started in 1964. Engines were three tail-mounted Rolls-Royce Speys. The Trident was the first airliner designed for automatic landing in bad visibility, and the first such landing on a passenger flight was in 1965, marking a major advance in airline regularity.

Later enlarged versions were built, but the similar-looking though larger Boeing 727 swept the board in sales. That reduction in size cost the company dearly. Inevitably BEA, and its successor British Airways, wanted a larger version, and even sought to buy Boeing 727s!

One problem was that Rolls-Royce could not wring much more from the Spey, so a desperate solution was adopted, fit a fourth engine in the tail! The engine chosen was the RB162, a little turbojet originally designed as a 'lift' engine for vertical take-off aircraft (and largely made of fibreglass, although there was less in the Trident version). This was used in the Trident 3b, on take-off only, creating an unpopular howl, but it worked.

Few other airlines bought Tridents, but one which did was Pakistan International. They soon sold them, to China, and this proved a lucky break, for China went on to buy 35 more, at least staving off total disaster. Altogether 117 Tridents were sold.

de Havilland Vampire and Venom
early jet fighters

The Vampire was the second British jet fighter to fly, in September 1943. Unlike the Meteor, de Havilland chose a single-engine design. The tail was mounted on twin tail booms, allowing a short fuselage and hence jet-pipe to be used to reduce power loss from the modest-thrust early engines (de Havilland Goblins).

Vampires were just too late to see war service but became standard equipment for many fighter and ground attack squadrons. No less than 3,268 were built, seeing service in numerous airforces throughout the world.

A trainer version appeared in 1950 and was the standard RAF advanced trainer from 1952 till 1967. For a time, the RAF used all-jet training, but later found it more economical to start on small propeller-driven aircraft after all.

Naval versions were built, a Vampire being the first jet ever to land on a carrier, on 3rd December 1945, flown by Lt. Cdr. Eric Brown. Another Vampire was flown by John Cunningham to a world height record of 59,942ft (18,270m) on 22nd March 1948. The aircraft was much modified and lightened – it was rumoured the pilot took a haircut to save weight!

The Venom, first flown in 1949, was a more advanced version with slightly swept wing leading edge and more powerful Ghost engine. Some served in Switzerland until the 1980s.

de Havilland Canada airliners

success story from Canada

The Canadian branch of de Havilland was formed in 1928 to make Moths. Large wartime commitments included Tiger Moths and notably Mosquitos. After the war the company embarked on its own designs. Every one has been a success, a claim few companies can make.

First were the Chipmunk trainer and Beaver 'bush' transport (1947). This single-engine high-wing design could be flown on wheels, floats, and skis and was ideally suited to Canadian needs. 1,717 were built including large orders for the American and British armies.

The larger Otter to similar layout followed, but more important was its derivative, the Twin Otter. This 19 passenger turboprop really put de Havilland Canada in the airliner business, some 700 being sold.

After a couple of fairly specialised military transports, the company tackled the bigger 50-seat four-turboprop 'Dash 7' (from the type number DHC-7). Its quietness allowed it to fly from many airports closed to jets.

The 'Dash 8' is the latest in this succeeful line. A 56-seater with two larger Pratt & Whitney Canada PW123 turboprops, some 370 have been sold. The company is now owned by the Bombardier group and no longer has any connection with British companies.

A Twin Otter serving with an Antarctic expedition was responsible for the naming of a range of hills.

Whilst flying in 'whiteout' conditions, the crew touched the top of some hills but were fortunate to have been able to climb away. The area was thereafter called the 'Touchdown Hills'.

---

de Havilland Canada Chipmunk

classic primary trainer

The little Chipmunk trainer first flew in 1946 and its excellent handling soon marked it out as the ideal Tiger Moth replacement. The RAF took 735 of the 1,232 built, the British machines being made at Chester.

It entered RAF service in 1950 and the last few were not retired until 1996, making it the longest-serving RAF aeroplane ever. Among early pilots trained was the Duke of Edinburgh in 1952.

Dewoitine D.520
France's best wartime fighter

Last of a line of fine fighters and airliners designed by Emile Dewoitine, the D.520 with its Hispano engine was almost in the Spitfire class.

It was the best French fighter in 1940, but alas there were not enough to stop the invaders. Vichy forces took over the stock of D.520 and production of new ones, so Allied pilots now found themselves opposed by this fine fighter. In the final twist, when France was freed the survivors were then flown by Free French pilots.

Did some individual aeroplanes serve first with the Allies, then against them, and finally with them again?

Dornier Do 17 and 217
'Flying Pencils' – Luftwaffe medium bombers

The Do 17 flew as a mail-carrier and 6-seat transport in 1934. So cramped was the passenger cabin that it was widely believed that the supposed transport role was a facade for a bomber. Actually, it seems it really was designed as a transport after all! When its unsuitability as an airliner was recognised, the Do 17 was stored and forgotten.

Almost by chance it was resurrected when a former Lufthansa pilot working on requirements for bombers remembered the Do 17. The Do 17 became one of the standard Luftwaffe bombers. It was first tried in that testing-ground of German equipment and tactics, the Spanish civil war. Later it became one of the most unwelcome visitors to Britain.

Its long, slender fuselage prompted the popular name 'the Flying Pencil'. Like most bombers designed prewar, it was inadequately armed, which partly accounts for its high loss rate, 192 being destroyed in the Battle of Britain, about 300 having been on strength at the beginning.

The Do 217 looked similar but was slightly larger. Some served as nightfighters and a few carried early air-launched guided missiles. One crew scored an historic success by sinking the Italian battleship Roma, which was about to transfer to the Allies, with a Fritz X guided bomb. It was a pointer to the future of warfare.

Dornier Do 335 Pfeil
astonishing 'push-pull' fighter

One of the fastest piston-engine aeroplanes ever flown, the Pfeil (Arrow) used two 1,900 hp DB603 engines, one mounted in the nose and the other in the tail. This created much less drag than a normal wing-mounted twin-engine layout.

First flown in 1943, speeds of 474 mph (764 kph) were recorded. To avoid the rear propeller shredding the pilot if he had to escape, the propeller and fin could be jettisoned, and there was even an early ejector seat fitted. Pfeils reached the squadrons near the end of the war and several Allied pilots saw the unusual fighters, but there is no record of any being involved in combat.

Dornier flying-boats
most successful marine aircraft till World War Two

Claude Dornier, one of the pioneers of stressed-skin metal construction, flew the first Wal flying-boat in 1922. It used two engines in a tandem 'push-pull' arrangement on a 'parasol' wing (one mounted on a strut above the fuselage).

A characteristic was the use of 'sponsons', broad floats projecting from the fuselage. To evade a ban on making aeroplanes in Germany, early Wals were produced in Italy. Many versions appeared, including a larger '10-tonne Wal' and inevitable military variants.

An interesting experiment was the use of Wals for South Atlantic mail services. The flying-boat was catapulted from a liner when within range of its destination.

So successful was the design that serious thought was given to building modernised versions post-war, and a turboprop version was flown as late as 1983.

Perhaps Dornier became overconfident after the success of the Wal, for his next flying-boat was as big a failure as the Wal had been a success. The colossal 12-engine Do X just staggered into the air in 1929, but it was pressed to exceed 1,000-1,500 feet. The great beast was underpowered and a change of engines was to little avail. However, it did set a world record by carrying 169 people, including 9 stowaways.

One long-distance flight was performed, from Friedrichshafen to New York, but the time was unimpressive – 9 months. (Yes, it did fly rather than taxi there!). Three of the giants were built but scrapped as unusable.

Dornier post-war aeroplanes

Dornier restarted in Spain to avoid restrictions on aircraft building in Germany, but later moved back to their homeland. At first single-engine utilities were built, the Do 25 and 26, but the line expanded into light airliners such as the Do 228 of today.

An interesting diversion was the Do 31 vertical take-off jet transport flown in 1967. With two Bristol Pegasus vectored-thrust engines and 8 Rolls-Royce RB162 lift engines it was technically successful but hideously expensive and equally hideously noisy.

Wildlife specialist Michael Grzimek flew a Do27 for his work in Africa. After losing a wheel, he and three passengers endured a long wait while he circled over Nairobi to use up fuel.

After landing without injury, all four remarked that they had seen four newly dug graves in a cemetery below, but each had felt it wiser to keep silent!

Sadly Grzimek was later killed when the aeroplane crashed after colliding with a griffon vulture.

Douglas A-1 Skyraider
propeller-driven stalwart of Korea and Vietnam

Just too late for World War Two, the piston-engine Skyraider first flew in 1945 but came into its own in Korea and Vietnam. So useful was it for ground attack duties that it remained in production till 1957, by which time 3,180 had been built.

The seemingly obsolete Skyraider often proved more versatile than glamorous jets, and serious thought was given to restarting manufacture in 1965. On one occasion in Vietnam Skyraiders shot down a MiG-17 jet.

VALOUR IN VIETNAM

Skyraider pilot Bernard Fisher saw a colleague forced down on an airfield surrounded by Vietcong.

Almost suicidally he landed, somehow crammed his stricken colleague into the single-seater cockpit with him and took off, all under intense fire.

Douglas A-4 Skyhawk
outstanding lightweight jet fighter

Most military aircraft come out above their intended weights, but designer Ed Heinemann built the little Skyhawk at under half the weight specified by the US Navy! First flight of the Skyhawk, variously called Heinemann's Hot-rod or Tinkertoy, was in June 1954. It was to remain in production for 25 years, during which time 2,980 were made.

The engine was generally a Pratt & Whitney J52, although early examples used the Wright J65 (licence Sapphire). Effectiveness in action was proven in Vietnam, and by Israel in its usual devastating way in 1973, while in 1982 British forces saw what determined Argentine pilots could do with Skyhawks despite sophisticated missile defences. Many nations continue to fly this still effective 40-year-old design.

Douglas A-20 Boston
fine medium bomber of World War Two

This twin-engine high-wing bomber entered service with the RAF in 1941. The RAF machines had been ordered by France, and before RAF service a French eccentricity of the time had to be changed – the throttles were rigged in the opposite direction to everyone else!

Bostons and the similar Havoc nightfighters served well and were regarded as a major improvement on the Blenheims they replaced. 7,385 were built.

Its successor, the A-26 Invader with a new laminar-flow wing, proved outstanding in the last months of the war, again in Korea and yet again in Vietnam. The USAF kept some in service till 1972. Some are now used for firebombing – one Canadian company has 18.

LIGHTEN OUR DARKNESS

Some Havoc nightfighters were fitted with searchlights, the
Turbinlites. One was supposed to illuminate the enemy
aircraft leaving a partner to shoot it down.

Radar superceded the scheme.

Douglas Boston

The gunner had a set of controls in case the pilot was hit,
but there was a catch — how could the rearward-facing
gunner see where he was going?

Douglas DC-3 (Dakota)
classic transport of the piston era

Many in aviation consider the DC-3 to have been one of the finest
aeroplanes ever to have flown. So soundly was it designed that 60 years
later some hundreds are still flying.

The story of the DC (Douglas Commercial) airliners started with the first
flight of the DC-1 on 1st July, 1933. It nearly ended there, too, for just after
take-off both engines cut. Test pilot Carl Cover pushed the nose down and
the engines recovered, the process repeating itself each time he raised the
nose. By careful handling he possibly saved the future of the DC series.
The fault was due to an assembly error in the fuel system.

The DC-1 had been designed to meet a requirement from the airline TWA
for a trimotor airliner. Douglas thought they could meet the need more
efficiently with a twin, and the 12-passenger DC-1 proved them right. TWA
and other airlines ordered the slightly larger 14-seat DC-2. (The sole DC-1
was damaged beyond repair at Malaga in 1940).

The DC-2 flew in May 1934, entering service a week after first flight. It was
an immediate success with orders flowing in from around the world. The
Dutch airline KLM gave the DC-2 an early boost by entering one with mail
and a few intrepid passengers in the 1934 MacRobertson race from Britain
to Australia. The DC-2 came second, and first in a handicap section,
conceding place only to one of the specially built de Havilland Comet racers.

220 DC-2s were built, most with Wright Cyclone or Pratt & Whitney Hornet
engines, but a few used Bristol Pegasus engines which Douglas considered
the best of all. American Airways asked Douglas for an enlarged coast-to-
coast sleeper version. At first Douglas were reluctant to build it. How
pleased they must later have been that they were persuaded!

The 'Douglas Sleeper Transport' flew on 17th December 1935, but it was
the 21-seat day version, the immortal DC-3, which filled the skies of the
world. Engines were Wright Cyclones or (later much more commonly) Pratt
& Whitney Twin Wasps.

Here was the first airliner to make profits on passengers alone, without mail subsidy. It was largely due to the DC-3 that American airline traffic expanded five-fold between 1935 and 1941. Its then advanced design with careful attention to reducing drag, its immensely strong triple-spar wing with flaps, and variable-pitch propellers, would serve its owners for decades to come.

Wartime needs saw vastly expanded production. In the USAAF the peacetime DC-3 became the C-47, or less reverently the Gooney Bird, while the RAF christened it Dakota. Whatever they were called, they served in every theatre of war carrying paratroops, towing gliders, evacuating the wounded, bringing in supplies, and landing agents behind enemy lines.

Few aeroplanes earned more respect from their crews. 10,691 were built in the USA, about 3,500 in Russia as the Lisunov Li-2 (some with gun turrets) and 450 in Japan which omitted to pay the licence fee after 1941. Russia also received 707 under lend-lease but neglected to return them.

Postwar the DC-3 became the mainstay of airlines all over the world until it became gradually displaced on to lesser routes. Many a manufacturer spotted the large market for a 'DC-3 replacement', Some made good but many saw their so-called replacements outlived by the DC-3.

In the early months of the Berlin Airlift it was the unending streams of C-47s and Dakotas which sustained the beleagured citizens. Later the larger C-54 took the brunt of the work. A quite different enterprise was the first landing at the South Pole, in 1956, by a US Navy R4D (naval equivalent of the C-47).

In Vietnam the old warhorse was back, in a surprisingly aggressive way. Three sideways-facing machine-guns could be pointed by the wing-tip at the ground, giving a latterday broadside of great accuracy and devastating effect.

Douglas DC-3 Dakota –

60 Years Service, and Still Flying

Still the DC-3 flies on. The number still flying is unknown but is counted in hundreds – some believe it still exceeds 1,000. They carry freight, serve airforces, handle all kinds of aerial work, and yes, some still carry passengers 60 years after they first did so.

Some aircraft have flown around 100,000 hours and show few signs of wearing out. A few operators are fitting turbine engines, an investment which is worth-while only if they see many years of work ahead. There is therefore good reason to believe some of these fine aeroplanes will still be at work into the 21st century.

A Chinese-owned DC-3 had a wing damaged away from home base by Japanese bombs. No spare wing was available, but there was one for a DC-2. The wing root fittings were the same but it was 5 ft shorter. It was flown out under another DC-2 (a feat of flying in itself), fitted, and the hybrid flown home.

It was dubbed the DC-2$^1/_2$ – others suggested the Chinese call it the 'wun wing lo'.

HITCHING A LIFT

The DC-3/Dakota made an excellent glider tug. Hundreds participated at Arnhem and the Rhine landings. Gliders could even be 'snatched' from clearings without the tug landing. The tug pilot flew over the glider and picked up the tow-rope from a loop held up by cables – a tricky piece of flying.

In an epic flight, one Dakota towed a glider across the Atlantic. Perhaps strangest of all, one C-47 was itself adapted as a glider. The engine nacelles were faired over and it was claimed it proved more efficient than purpose-built gliders, but admirers of the Douglas transport will find that no surprise.

ROPING IN THE PASSENGERS

Captains of old airliners sometimes need to improvise to keep flying. An Indonesian DC-3 pilot had no intention of staying grounded when an engine starter failed at a remote airstrip. He looped a rope over a propeller blade and deployed the able-bodied passengers along its length.

At his command, a tug on the rope swung the propeller and brought the engine to life.

Douglas DC-4 to DC-7

piston rulers of the airways

These four-engined airliners dominated long-haul travel from 1942 till 1958. There were two DC-4s. The first, a large triple-fin affair, flew in 1938. It was intended as the last word in air travel at the time – there was even a bridal suite – but the airlines felt it too complex and costly.

It was bought by Japan and reportedly crashed; in fact it had not, but had been dismantled and used as basis for a bomber. Douglas later renumbered it DC-4E.

The later DC-4 became a classic. It first flew in 1942 as a military C-54 Skymaster. Engines were 4 Pratt & Whitney R2000. It became the standard USAAF long-haul transport for the rest of the war and some years afterwards.

The C-54 was the most important element of the Berlin airlift. 1,315 civil and military versions were built. The DC-4 airliner filled a major role until the later DC-6 appeared.

The Canadian company Canadair built a pressurised version with Rolls-Royce Merlins called the Canadair 4, or according to whichever airline used it, the North Star or Argonaut.

BOAC regarded the Argonaut as their principal airliner for some years, and despite high noise levels and frightening exhaust flames at night, many travellers of the time had surprisingly fond memories of this airliner.

Another variation on the DC-4 theme was a British car-ferry conversion, the Carvair of 1961. A swing nose admitted 5 cars with 22 passengers. The cockpit was placed above, Boeing 747 style. 21 were converted but although the car-ferry business seemed to be booming it had passed its peak and would soon disappear. But they made good general freighters.

The larger and pressurised DC-6 followed in 1946. Early service was marred by two in-flight fires leading to the type being grounded, but the series became highly successful. The DC-6 itself was lengthened in 1951 to become the DC-6A (freight), DC-6B (passengers) and DC-6C (mixed).

The DC-6B, seating up to 102, is often considered the best of all the four-engine Douglas piston airliners. A few of the 704 built fly on today.

The yet further stretched DC-7 appeared in 1953. Extra power came from Wright R-3350 turbo-compound engines, but the complex nature of these engines and their demanding maintenance led to most DC-7s being retired before the older DC-4s and DC-6s. Ultimate in the series was the longer-span DC-7C, the 'Seven Seas', which had transatlantic range.

BOAC bought a fleet pending delayed delivery of their Britannias. 338 of the DC-7 series were built.

The DC-6 had square windows, whereas those on the older DC-4 were round. Some airlines still flying DC-4s tried to fool knowledgeable travellers by painting black squares round the windows to make them look like DC-6s!

At least one DC-7 found a most unexpected use after its airline days were over – for racing! What a sight it must have been, rounding the pylons in a steep turn.

THE BERLIN AIRLIFT – OPERATION PLAINFARE

Russia closed all surface links with Berlin in June 1948. The Allies resolved on the unprecedented task of supplying the entire city by air. At first the load was borne by USAF C-47s and RAF Dakotas, Yorks, Sunderland flying-boats and civilian transports. Later it was the C-54, the military DC-4, which really took the strain.

So tightly scheduled were the landings that a pilot making a missed approach could not be slotted back into the traffic stream; he had to fly back to his loading airfield.

On the ground, too, every effort was made to save seconds on loading and unloading. When Berlin's Tempelhof airport was nearing capacity, a new solution was proposed: build another airfield, and astonishingly, it was ready within three months!

Inevitably there were incidents when men worked under such pressure. An RAF pilot found his Dakota sluggish to take off and handle in the air – not surprisingly when it was later found to have been loaded with seven tons instead of its normal three.

By extraordinary effort the city was sustained, notably with coal even more than food, and the blockade was lifted in May 1949.

A C-54 pilot on the Berlin Airlift saw the children lacked pleasures like chocolates and arranged to drop some, against regulations. So the recipients would recognise him, he arranged to waggle the wings as a signal.

Soon he was 'rumbled' by authority, but far from being disciplined his initiative started 'Operation Vittals', collecting such luxuries throughout the airforce and distributing them to Berlin children.

THE MISSING AIRLINER

The DC-4, DC-6 and DC-7 made a long series from 1942 till 1958. Some readers might ask, was there a DC-5? Indeed there was, but only 12 were built. It was a twin-engine high-wing airliner similar to the Douglas Boston bomber.

Orders were coming in before the war, including a fleet for the prewar British Airways, but most were cancelled due to hostilities and Douglas found higher priorities than the DC-5.

Douglas jet airliners, DC-8 to DC-10

some of the world's finest jetliners

Despite dominating the piston-engine airliner business, Douglas took a huge gamble in launching the four-jet DC-8; the capital at risk was more than the value of the company.

The DC-8 somewhat resembled the rival Boeing 707, which had the advantage of starting earlier. Both firms anxiously awaited Pan American's choice, for whichever was not chosen would probably be abandoned. Finally Juan Trippe, wily chairman of Pan American, ordered both!

First flight was on 30th May 1958. 294 'standard' DC-8s were built, though with variations in seating and range. Engines were Pratt & Whitney JT3s, JT4s or later the turbofan JT3D, while 3 airlines chose the Rolls-Royce Conway.

In 1966 the 'Super Sixty' series appeared, some stretched by as much as 36ft (11m) to seat up to 259 passengers. Here the DC-8 scored over the Boeing 707, for the latter could not readily be lengthened. Many of these DC-8s remain in service, some re-engined with CFM56 large-fan engines. The DC-9 had its two Pratt & Whitney JT8D engines mounted in the then fashionable tail position. It first flew in February 1965 and entered service just 9 months later.

Early DC-9s carried 90 passengers, but it is a reflection of the soundness of design that current versions (now sold under MacDonnell-Douglas type numbers like MD-80) carry double that number. Some 2,000 of all versions have been sold, making it one of the most successful of all airliners.

The DC-10, first flown in 1970, is a wide-body trijet seating up to 380. Despite the success of the DC-9, such were the development costs that even Douglas could not handle them alone and merged with MacDonnell in 1967.

The company's reputation and that of the DC-10 was harmed by a series of accidents. In 1972 a cargo door detached leaving the hold unpressurised. Pressurisation loads caused the cabin floor to collapse jamming some of the controls. By fine airmanship the captain landed safely. Regrettably corrective action which should have followed did not, and two years later a Turkish DC-10 suffered the same problem, this time killing all 346 on board.

A later accident at Chicago when an engine detached further tarnished the type's image. However although production virtually closed at one stage, the updated MD-11 successor is selling in reasonable numbers, but sadly the famous 'DC' line has ended.

In 1960 a Rolls-Royce Conway powered DC-8 made aviation history in a minor way – as the first airliner to exceed Mach 1.

Douglas SBD Dauntless
one of the principal American wartime carrier aircraft

The SBD, first flown in 1938, could be flown as a conventional or dive bomber. 5,938 were made and are claimed to have sunk more Japanese shipping than any other type.

At the Battle of Midway, Dauntlesses decisively swung the battle by sinking 4 Japanese carriers, but at the high loss rate of 40 out of 128 deployed.

DAUNTLESS MACHINE, DAUNTLESS MEN

The losses at Midway illustrate just how much courage those carrier crews needed.

Even in peacetime it is a particularly demanding type of flying, but in war it requires bravery of a high order, for the chances of rescue from the sea in a battle are poor.

Douglas World Cruiser
first round the world

Four aircraft set out on 17th March, 1926, flown by Army Air Service crews. Two arrived back 175 days later, together with a replacement which had joined part way.

One of the others crashed in Alaska, the crew surviving an epic 10-day trek in a blizzard. Another ditched near the Faroes.

Embraer
success story from Brazil

Who would have imagined a few years ago that the standard RAF trainer of the 1990s would be a Brazilian design? The Tucano trainer is just one of the resounding successes from this relative newcomer to aeroplane design (RAF Tucanos were built by Shorts).

Embraer was formed in 1970, but already the first design was flying, the 19-seat Bandeirante twin-turboprop transport, which has sold all over the world.

The Tucano followed in 1980 (over 600 sold), and the 30-seat Brazilia, with over 300 sales to date, in 1983. Embraer has been an astonishing success from a country with such severe economic problems.

English Electric Canberra
excellent medium bomber

The twin-jet Canberra, designed by 'Teddy' Petter, was first flown by Roland Beamont on 13th May, 1949. Friday the 13th it might have been, but it was far from unlucky. Engines were two Rolls-Royce Avons.

The Canberra entered service in 1951 and has remained in RAF service ever since, although in 1995 the end seems near. This makes it the longest-serving large RAF aeroplane ever, and one of the most versatile.

From the outset the Canberra showed its paces, setting 22 world records including the first double Atlantic crossing in a day, in 1952. Canberras were used operationally in Malaya, Egypt, and in Borneo. Many Canberras were exported, and licence production started in Australia and America. The latter were made by Martin as the B-57 with Wright J65 engines (licence-built Armstrong Siddeley Sapphires).

B-57s served in Vietnam until 1969. Some highly developed B-57 versions appeared, including a high-altitude reconnaissance version with 122ft span (37m) wing, almost double that of a standard Canberra, and there was even a 4-engine B-57. 1,376 Canberras and B-57s were built.

> *After a heavy snowfall, a line of parked Canberras took on an undignified stance – the weight of snow on the tailplane made them sit on their tails.*

English Electric Lightning
Mach 2 fighter

Based on early studies by Teddy Petter and developed by 'Freddie' Page, the Lightning used a 60° swept wing with the two Rolls-Royce Avons mounted above each other but staggered in the fuselage. First flight was in August 1954 as the P1 with Sapphire engines, but mainly due to political delays it was not until 1960 that production Lightnings entered service.

The Lightning was the first British Mach 2 fighter. It gave excellent service, although the accident rate was on the high side. Export orders were secured for Saudi Arabia and Kuwait, but had there been political support for a ground attack version the potential sales could have been several times as large for this fine aeroplane.

Eurofighter 2000
the mainstay of future European defence?

Britain, Germany, Italy and Spain have joined forces on this programme which, if politicians and finances permit, will be the centre of these nations' defences from the year 2000 onwards.

First flight was in March 1994. Engines are two Eurojet EJ200s, likewise built by a four-nation consortium. Like most new fighter designs, the Eurofighter is made deliberately unstable but controlled by computers. Without the computers it would instantly tumble out of control, but the reward is an agility which would otherwise be impossible.

Fairchild A-10 Thunderbolt II
tanks beware!

The ugly A-10 was designed for battlefield support and as a 'tankbuster' in particular. First flown in 1972, lessons had been learned from Vietnam that combat aeroplanes may be hit!

It was designed to take severe damage and still survive. For similar reasons the two General Electric TF34 engines are mounted in the least vulnerable place, above and behind the wing. 825 of these potent machines were made.

Its unaesthetic appearance has given it the unofficial name 'Warthog'. The A-10 proved highly effective in the 1991 Gulf war against Iraq. It was no fault of the aircraft that it was involved in a tragic attack on a British army unit.

Fairchild C-82 and C-119 Packet, or Flying Boxcars
capacious freighters

The C-82 was just too late for World War Two but proved invaluable in the Berlin Airlift, and again with the later C-119 in Korea and Vietnam.

These freighters used a twin-boom layout, enabling large doors to be fitted at the rear of the fuselage. This made it the most versatile American freighter before the Lockheed Hercules. In Vietnam it was used as a 'gunship', with 4 sideways-pointing machine-guns, aimed by pointing the wing-tip at the target in a tight turn. Results were devastating.

The Indian Airforce fitted a Bristol Orpheus jet on top of their C-119s to boost power in mountainous areas. These aircraft played a major part in dropping paratroops against Pakistan, leading to the independence of Bangladesh.

Fairey Battle
misconceived light bomber

The Battle looked modern when it appeared in 1936, but not even the legendary Rolls-Royce Merlin could give this single-engine bomber enough speed, and with just one defensive gun there was only one likely outcome to any attack by an enemy fighter.

The Battle had one moment of glory – on 20th September 1939 a rear gunner shot down the first German aircraft of the war, a Bf109. Otherwise losses were appalling; the first two air VCs of the war were awarded to Battle pilots, both posthumous.

The Battles were belatedly withdrawn late in 1940, most ending their days as trainers, target tugs, or engine test-beds.

Fairey Delta Two
world speed record holder

The first Fairey Delta was a small, portly research machine, designed to be launched from a ramp with rocket assistance. It never did so, which was probably as well since its handling was dangerous. By contrast the Fairey Delta 2 was a thoroughbred.

On 10th March 1956 this slender delta set a new world speed record of 1,132mph (1,822kph), flown by Peter Twiss. Britain could have used it as the basis for an excellent fighter, but almost unbelievably allowed Dassault in France to test it, inspiring the world-wide success of the Mirage deltas.

The FD2 had one more role to play; rebuilt as the Bristol 221 it tested the ogival wing shape used on Concorde.

Fairey Firefly
naval fighter

Fairey had already built one World War Two carrier fighter, the two-seat and rather slow Fulmar. The Firefly was much better, and served particularly well against Japanese positions towards the end of the war.

The Firefly was one of the principal naval types in Korea, and it was considered good enough to remain in production until 1956, well into the jet era. The engine was a Rolls-Royce Griffon.

Fairey Fox
the bomber that outflew contemporary fighters

Richard Fairey had formed his company in 1915. Two years later he is credited with making the first wing flaps. Over 1,000 of a long series of Fairey III biplanes were built. They made many notable flights including the first round Australia, but by the mid-1920s Fairey needed a new design.

The 1924 Fox was a leap forward in performance. This single-engine bomber outpaced every fighter with its 150mph (241kph) speed. The engine was a Curtiss D-12 which Fairey wanted to build but was denied official permission.

Despite its advanced design, the Fox brought little reward for Fairey; sales were limited to one squadron for the RAF and a Belgian order.

Fairey Rotodyne
advanced convertible helicopter

The Rotodyne, flown in 1957, was a most advanced, almost visionary 40-passenger transport. Forward power was provided by two Napier Eland turboprops mounted on short wings driving conventional propellers.

For take-off or hover the rotor was driven by small tip-mounted jets, but once in cruising flight the rotor was unpowered. Performance was excellent and several class records were taken.

In 1960 Fairey became part of Westland, and a combination of lower interest by the new owner, high operating costs, and the fearsome noise of the tip jets led to cancellation in 1962.

Fairey Swordfish

perhaps the most improbable success of World War Two

The Swordfish torpedo bomber, designed by Marcel Lobelle and first flown in 1934, was already obsolete by the outbreak of war. Nevertheless astonishing successes were achieved. In November 1940 a low-level attack on Taranto harbour left 3 Italian battleships and several other ships sunk or crippled for the loss of two Swordfish.

In 1941 two series of attacks were made on the battleship Bismark. On the last attempt, after an unfortunate mistaken attack on HMS Sheffield, one torpedo crippled Bismark's steering gear, allowing British capital ships to sink her.

Many less famous successes were recorded – in one case 4 ships were sunk with 3 torpedoes. However, these results were possible only with almost unbelievable courage and fortitude – missions often involved long hours in open cockpits.

Fairey Swordfish – Unlikely Terror of the Axis Fleets

Inevitably sometimes these slow biplanes took heavy losses, as when Eugene Esmonde led 6 Swordfish against German cruisers in the English Channel. Every Swordfish was lost, and Esmonde was awarded a posthumous VC.

Popularly known as the 'Stringbag', the Swordfish was powered by a Bristol Pegasus engine. 2,396 were made, and it was one of the few aeroplanes in service at the beginning and end of the war. Strangely enough it even outlived its intended successor, the closed-cockpit Albacore.

> *Swordfish pilot Simon Borrett had good reason to thank the strength and flying qualities of his aircraft. Whilst flying in cloud his wing hit a barrage-balloon cable.*
>
> *The wing was partly severed and he was swung round facing whence he had come, but the 'Stringbag' kept on flying.*

Farmans

favourites of the French pioneers

Brothers Henry and Maurice Farman each set up separate aeroplane building companies in 1909. They merged again in 1915. Early Farmans were improved Voisin 'box-kite' designs, with better controls.

They were among the most popular trainers for pre-1914 British and French pilots. Wartime Farman designs were inhibited by French government specifications and they were generally outclassed.

Post-war French airline services were largely based on the twin-engined Goliath. The passenger cabin had forward-facing windows in the nose, doubtless giving a panoramic view but disconcerting in the not uncommon event of imminent mishap. The Farman company was nationalised in 1937.

Fiat G91
NATO's lightweight fighter

Fiat had a long history of aircraft building dating back to 1914. In World War Two Fiat designs tended to be outclassed, the CR42 probably being the last fighter biplane to be produced in the world, up till 1944.

The G91 was designed to meet a NATO specification for a lightweight fighter, supposedly to be used by all member states. Politicians do not agree that easily, and only Italy and Germany bought the G91, followed second-hand by Portugal.

First flown in 1956, the G91 proved a most capable fighter, its abilities being well demonstrated by the Italian aerobatic team for some years. The engine was a Bristol Orpheus.

Fieseler Storch
Germany's army co-operation aeroplane

The Storch (Stork) had outstanding take-off and landing capabilities. In still air it could be airborne in 215ft (65m). Gerhard Fieseler produced the first Storch in 1936. It was a high-wing monoplane with high-lift flaps and slots, a long spindly undercarriage, and a 240 hp Argus engine.

The Storch was widely used for observation over Allied lines, for staff transport, and as an ambulance.

STORCH SPECTACULARS

When Italian dictator Mussolini was imprisoned by the Allies in a supposedly impregnable mountain fortress, a German commando unit plucked him away using the almost unique ability of the Storch to land almost anywhere.

In the last days of Berlin, the legendary woman pilot Hanna Reitsch flew a Storch into the city at night under Russian fire. She seemed to lead a charmed life and beat the suicidal odds.

Focke-Wulf 190

best German piston-engine fighter of World War Two

The Fw190 came as a nasty shock to Allied pilots when it appeared in 1941 and outclassed the latest Spitfires. In fact it should have been no surprise, for the 190 was first flown in June 1939 and shown publicly before the war.

The 190 was designed by Kurt Tank and powered by a BMW radial engine of 1,800 hp and upwards. This too added to early disbelief, for many in Britain felt high performance to be impossible from a radial engine, but the new fighter was real enough and a serious threat.

Later, new marks of Spitfire matched the 190, helped by a German pilot obligingly landing one in South Wales, believing himself to be over France. This gift resulted in full evaluation of its performance. However the 190 was always held in great respect. Nearly 20,000 were made.

DEADLY MISTLETOE

The Mistel (Mistletoe) comprised a piloted Fw190 mounted atop an obsolete bomber packed with explosives. The pilot flew both aircraft until the bomber was released towards its target.

Some successes were achieved on the Russian front.

In 1943 a unit was formed of pilots who had committed some flying 'offence'. They signed pledges to destroy at least one Allied aircraft per sortie, if not by gunfire then by ramming.

The Fw190s were strengthened for the 'ramm-staffel'. In practice, and perhaps unsurprisingly, ramming was quite rare.

Focke-Wulf Fw200 Condor

'Scourge of the Atlantic'

The Fw200, first flown by designer Kurt Tank in 1937, started as a 26-seat four-engine airliner. Several noteworthy long-distance flights were performed, including non-stop from Berlin to New York in 25 hours and to Tokyo in 46 hours with 3 stops. The Tokyo triumph was marred by loss of the aircraft on the return.

A few entered airline service, and some performed the ignoble duty of carrying Hitler and other top Nazis. On the outbreak of war production switched to bomber, minelaying and maritime patrol versions.

Allied seamen loathed the Condors shadowing the convoys, reporting their positions but keeping just out of gun range. Later, convoys were protected by Hurricanes catapulted from merchant ships. These shot down a number of Condors but the pilot had to ditch and hope a ship could rescue him. Finally, small escort carriers saw off the Condors.

For all its notoriety, only 276 Condors were made, and many were lost in landing accidents. The structure was not really strong enough for military duties. Engines were BMW or Bramo radials.

Fokker DVII
best German fighter of World War One

The DVII, designed by Reinhold Platz, entered service in April 1918. Fast, manoeuvrable, and a good performer at altitude, the DVII is considered one of the best fighters of the war.

When the Armistice was signed, the DVIIs were ordered to be destroyed, but wily Anthony Fokker clandestinely moved all part-built aeroplanes and tooling to Holland where he resumed production.

Fokker Dr1 Triplane
legendary mount of the 'Red Baron'

Famed as von Richthofen's steed for his later victories (most of his successes were in other types) and the one in which he met his end, the Dr1 was made in quite small numbers and had drawbacks.

The triplane entered service in 1917 but was fairly slow and had limited endurance. Where it scored was in manoeuvrability, and in expert hands it was devastating.

Fokker EIII Eindekker
1915 scourge of the Western front

A French pilot, Roland Garros, had fitted deflector plates to the propeller of his aircraft so that a machine-gun could fire through the propeller. He was shot down and when Anthony Fokker saw the metal plates he improved on the idea with his 'interrupter gear', which prevented the gun firing into the propeller.

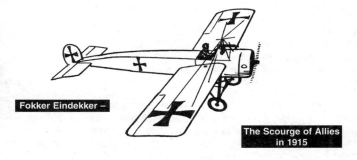

Fokker Eindekker –

The Scourge of Allies in 1915

The Eindekker ('monoplane') reigned supreme from August 1915 till early 1916. Allied pilots called this period the 'Fokker Scourge', which ended when effective Allied fighters appeared.

Fokker F.VII series
world-beating airliners of the 1920s

The single-engine 8-passenger F.VII flew in 1924. It was a high-wing monoplane of a type which became a Fokker trademark. More important was the tri-motor F.VII-3m, flown in 1925. It was entered for, and won, a reliability trial run by Henry Ford in America.

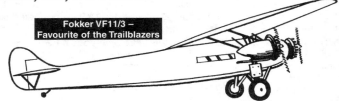

Fokker VF11/3 –
Favourite of the Trailblazers

The trials aeroplane, now named 'Josephine Ford', became the first to reach the North Pole, in 1926, flown by Richard Byrd and Floyd Bennett. The Polar flight was the first of many outstanding flights by the Fokker tri-motors. Most famous of all was Charles Kingsford-Smith's 'Southern Cross', which among other flights made the first across the Pacific, in 1928. 'Southern Cross' was an enlarged version, the F.VIIb-3m.

Airlines throughout the world flew Fokker tri-motors. They were also built in America and Britain, the latter as the Avro Ten. Their day ended when the American stressed-skin metal Boeing 247 and Douglas DC-2 swept all before them. Anthony Fokker realised their supremacy and took out a licence to build the Douglas airliners, but war forstalled him.

Fokker post-war airliners
– a world-wide success story

Fokker were one of the few to succeed in building a 'Douglas DC-3 replacement'. The company astutely saw the future lay in turbine power and equipped their high-wing F.27 Friendship with two Rolls-Royce Dart turboprops. It first flew in 1955.

The F.27 became a world-wide success with over 700 sold, helped by the American company Fairchild building it under licence. In the mid-1980s a modernised version, the Fokker 50, appeared with Pratt & Whitney Canada PW125 engines, and this still sells in small numbers. Thus essentially the same design has been made for 40 years, a fine achievement by Fokker.

Fokker moved into jets with the 100-seat F-28 Fellowship in 1969, with two tail-mounted Rolls-Royce Spey Juniors. Sales were steady if unspectacular, but with the modernised F100, with the larger Tay engine, Fokker won some large orders in the demanding American market.

However, times are tough for airliner builders and despite the excellence of the product and a fine reputation for service support, the historic Fokker company became insolvent in March, 1996.

Folland Gnat

lightweight fighter and mount of the Red Arrows

Designer 'Teddy' Petter sought to break away from the spiral of ever heavier and more expensive combat aircraft. His little Gnat succeeded admirably, although never bought by the RAF as a fighter.

The Gnat flew in 1955 (a lower-powered prototype, the Midge, flew the previous year). The RAF did buy it as an advanced trainer, and the famous Red Arrows formation team started on Gnats and continued to astonish the crowds with them until the present Hawks arrived. Red Arrows Gnats had faster control response than the standard trainer.

Finland and India flew Gnat fighters, the latter country building large numbers and developing it further as the Ajeet. Gnats performed well in action against Pakistan, vindicating Petter's idea of the lightweight fighter.

> *Communication is vital in flying, but even the best can err under stress.*
> *A Gnat was in trouble and the pilot ordered to eject.*
> *Another pilot, hearing the 'eject' order and believing it was for him, abandoned a perfectly serviceable Gnat.*

Ford Trimotor

sturdy airliner of the 1920s

Henry Ford was keen to add aviation to his car empire. He bought an existing company, the Stout Metal Airplane Company (Stout was its founder's name, not a reference to robustness), and had a series of trimotors built. They resembled the Fokker FVII-3m series but differed in using 'Alclad' metal construction instead of wood.

The Fords were strong and could even be looped, presumably without passengers aboard. From the mid-1920s until the Boeing 247 and Douglas DC-2 appeared, the 'Tin Goose' was the mainstay of American air travel.

A few were still flying in the 1980s, and some devotees of the type actually built a modernised version in 1975 as the Bushmaster 2000.

FIRST TO THE POLES

A Ford Trimotor achieved the distinction of making the first flight to the South Pole. Commander Richard Byrd, with three crew, reached the desolate spot on 28th November, 1929.

Three years earlier Byrd had flown over the North Pole in a Fokker tri-motor. Thus one man is credited with the first flights over both geographic poles.

General Dynamics F-111
first 'swing-wing' in service

The F-111 had a troublesome start. Intended to serve both the USAF and US Navy, the latter soon pulled out when the aeroplane was seen to be grossly overweight. The RAF ordered 50 but cancelled them, while Australia ordered 24 but refused to take delivery for 5 years while political arguments raged.

The F-111 first flew in December 1964 on the power of two Pratt & Whitney TF30 turbofans. It was the first variable geometry, or 'swing-wing' aircraft to enter service. The wing is almost straight to give low flying speeds for take-off and landing, but sharply swept for high speeds. Another innovation was that in emergency the entire crew compartment detaches and descends by parachute. Its job is still not finished, for it then acts as a refuge against bad weather.

Yet another advance was in the use of 'terrain-following radar', allowing the F-111 to fly fast and low even in cloud or at night. Similar electronic systems have since been fitted to most high-performance attack aircraft.

The F-111 entered service in 1967. An early deployment to Vietnam was discouraging, with 3 lost in accidents in 55 missions. However in a later deployment in 1972 the F-111 acquitted itself admirably. 18 F-111s were used to attack the Libyan capital, Tripoli, in 1986. Only 562 were built, but for all its early problems and controversy it caused, it is now considered an excellent aeroplane and current plans are for it to remain in service till around 2010.

> *Before this first 'swing-wing' aeroplane flew, there was much argument as to which way the wing sweep lever should move. Some wanted it to move forward with increasing sweep-back, similar to a throttle moving forward to increase speed, while others preferred the lever to move forward as the wings swept forward. The first view prevailed.*

General Dynamics F-16 Fighting Falcon
trendsetting fighter with electronic control

American forces learned a hard lesson in Vietnam. Fighters built for high speeds of over Mach 2 lost that speed rapidly when turning in combat and more manoeuvrable opponents would often prevail.

The F-16 achieved unprecedented manoeuvrability by using a 'fly-by-wire' control system. The aeroplane is unstable but controlled electronically, providing remarkable agility – 9g turns can be made. The principle has since become widely used on combat aircraft.

First flown in 1974, the F-16 won a 'fly-off' competition and went on to secure large orders from the USAF and from 4 European countries, referred to at the time as 'the sale of the century'. Orders from all sources exceed 3,500, making it one of the most successful jet combat aircraft ever made.

The engine is a single Pratt & Whitney F-100 or General Electric F-110 turbofan. Although designed as an air superiority fighter, the F-16 has become even more widely used for ground attack. Even a single-engine machine like the F-16 carries a heavier load than the great 4-engine bombers of World War Two. Some 13,500 missions were flown in the 1991 Gulf War.

The official name is often seen as clumsy (the French Dassault company had reserved 'Falcon' on its own), and the name 'Viper' is widely used, or more colloquially 'Electric Jet' in a reference to the fly-by-wire controls.

PRECISION ATTACK

Israel showed the devastating effectiveness of the F-16 in using 8 such machines to destroy the Iraqi nuclear reactor at Osirak in 1981.

Israel was much criticised, but who would doubt now that she did the world a good turn?

Officially the F-16 first flew on 2nd February, 1974. In fact it had already flown on 21st January, unintentionally! During high-speed taxi runs, tailplane damage occurred and caused instability.

Test pilot Phil Oestricher made an instant decision to take off, and completed a safe circuit.

HOW MANY ENGINES?

What is there to choose between a single-engine combat aircraft like the F-16 and a twin such as the Tornado?

The single is cheaper, and usually more manoeuvrable thanks to its lighter weight. The twin can carry more equipment and is widely thought to be safer.

In practice the safety argument is less significant than is often supposed. Certainly fewer aircraft are lost when there are two engines, but on cost grounds this is offset by the difference in purchase price and operating cost.

If this sounds callous, what about the pilots? Statistically, the fatality rate is hardly affected by the number of engines. Fatal accidents tend to involve collisions, flying into the ground, or loss of control. A simple power loss generally gives times to eject and is rarely fatal.

Gloster E28/39
first British jet

The E28/39 was the culmination of years of work by jet engine pioneer Frank Whittle, struggling against official scepticism, lack of funds, and his own duties as an RAF officer. The E28/39 was a research aeroplane to test the jet engine.

The first British Jet – The Gloster E28/39

The clumsy type number reflects the year of its specification (1939) and the project number in that year. The name Pioneer was allocated but not widely used. The engine was a Whittle W.1.

Gerry Sayer made the first flight on 15th May, 1941. Poor weather delayed take-off until 7.35 pm; the tension may be imagined.

At the time it was thought to be the first jet flight in the world; only later was it found that the Heinkel 178 had flown in 1939. Incredibly, no official film or photographs were taken of the historic event.

Two E28/39s were built. The second crashed, but the first is preserved in the Science Museum, London.

TRIBULATIONS OF A JET PIONEER

Frank Whittle (later Sir Frank) proposed using gas turbines for aircraft propulsion in 1928. He filed his jet engine patent in 1930. He was not alone in working on gas turbines, but he was the only one at the time to think of a pure jet – others still thought of driving propellers.

Lack of official support and his commitments as an RAF officer delayed his first engine trials until 1937. A further four years were to pass before the first flight of a Whittle jet, in the Gloster E28/39.

At last Air Ministry support grew and sceptics were converted, but his troubles were far from over. His company, Power Jets, were authorised to build experimental engines but Rover were given the job of setting up production.

Regrettably Rover made painfully slow progress. It was not until Ernest Hives of Rolls-Royce exchanged his company's tank engine factory, making adapted Merlins, for Rover's jet facilities that production really started moving.

The first operation British jets, Gloster Meteors, entered service in July 1944. They could have been ready several years earlier. It was fortunate that the muddle in Germany was matched by at least as much disarray in Germany!

Gloster Gladiator

last RAF biplane fighter

Last in a long line of Gloster biplane fighters, the Gladiator entered service as late as 1937, by which time it was already obsolete. Gladiators saw plenty of action, with the Chinese against Japanese invaders, with Finnish forces against Russia, and with the RAF early in World War Two.

It is claimed Gladiators scored 250 victories. One pilot alone, 'Pat' Pattle, managed 30, a fine achievement in a clearly outclassed fighter.

The most famous of the type were 3 Sea Gladiators, named 'Faith, Hope and Charity', the gallant pilots of which provided the sole defence of Malta for 3 weeks, keeping at bay the might of the Italian Air Force.

GLOSTERS OF GLOUCESTER

Originally the Gloucestershire Aircraft Company, the firm found export customers unable to spell or pronounce their name, so in 1926 changed it to the simpler 'Gloster'.

Gloster Javelin

Gloster's delta fighter

The last of the long Gloster line was the Javelin all-weather fighter. This big delta was powered by two Armstrong Siddeley Sapphires. The Javelin served the RAF from 1956 until 1967. A proposed successor was cancelled and historic Glosters closed in 1964.

Test pilot Gerry Sayer, on asked for his impressions of the E28/39 remarked "it is the only aeroplane in which I can watch the fuel gauge needle moving".

The Javelin was demanding to fly – it was almost impossible to recover from a stall. Two test pilots were killed during development, but Chief Test Pilot Bill Waterton managed to land his Javelin after losing both elevators, skillfully controlling the aeroplane using its variable incidence tailplane.

He was awarded a George Medal for this feat.

Gloster Meteor
only Allied jet to serve in World War Two.

Designer George Carter chose twin engines for the first British jet fighter because of the low thrust from the early jets. Regrettable delays to the engine programme postponed Michael Daunt's first flight until 5th March 1943, and even then the intended Rover units were not ready, the flight being made with Halford H.1s (de Havilland Goblins).

First deliveries of Meteors, with Rolls-Royce Wellands (Rolls-Royce had taken over from Rover) were made on 12th July 1944.These are considered the first jets in service, just beating the Messerschmitt 262.

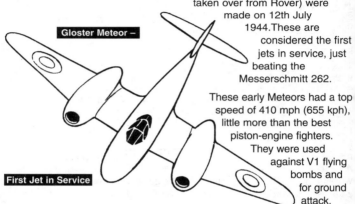

Gloster Meteor –

First Jet in Service

These early Meteors had a top speed of 410 mph (655 kph), little more than the best piston-engine fighters. They were used against V1 flying bombs and for ground attack.

Later Meteors became the principal RAF front-line fighters until the mid-1950s, equipping no less than 74 squadrons. 3,545 were built, including two-seat trainers and nightfighters which were made by Armstrong Whitworth. All except the first mark used Rolls-Royce Derwent engines.

The 'Meatbox' was widely exported and was well regarded. Meteors twice took the world speed record. On 7th November 1945 Gp. Capt. Hugh Wilson reached 606 mph (975 kph), while Gp. Capt. 'Teddy' Donaldson raised it to 616 mph (990 kph) on 7th September 1946, just failing to reach the 1,000 kph much sought after in Europe at the time.

Another landmark in aviation history was the first turboprop powered flight, on 20th September 1945. This Meteor was flown by Eric Greenwood, the engines being Rolls-Royce Trents, rudimentary conversions of Derwents with gearboxes.

In Korea, Australian units shot down 3 MiG-15s with their Meteors. However by then the Meteor was no real match for the swept-wing fighters and losses were heavy. Operational service with the RAF ended in 1961, but some remained flying overseas until at least 1970.

> *Gloster built a demonstrator Meteor at company expense. During a sales tour a Belgian pilot crashed it.*
>
> *When the wreckage was shipped back to Britain, customs officers delayed its entry because 'it was not in the same condition as when it left the country'.*

Gothas
1917 scourge of London

These twin-engine bombers raided London 27 times over about a year, starting in May 1917. Compared with the devastating raids of the next war, damage and casualties were light, but the raids still provoked a public and political outcry. The very formation of the RAF as a separate service was largely to meet this pressure.

The Gothas were actually far from invulnerable, some 60 being lost, 36 of these being in accidents, for the structure was liable to collapse on landing.

Grumman F4F Wildcat and F6F Hellcat
the naval fighting felines

First flown in 1937, the Wildcat was one of the most important carrier-borne fighters of World War Two. It was a mid-wing monoplane with the wheels retracting into the fuselage in a way which became a Grumman hallmark. Another company innovation was the ingenious wing-folding mechanism which stowed the wings alongside the fuselage.

At first the US Navy rejected the F4F in favour of the rival Brewster Buffalo. How bitterly they were to regret their choice! The Buffalo was a disaster. Grumman persisted with the F4F, which in 1940 entered service first with the Royal Navy, who used the name Martlet. Later, after the US Navy adopted the name Wildcat the Royal Navy followed suit.

The 1942 F6F Hellcat started as an improved F4F, but as often happens ended up as a new aeroplane.

The importance of the Hellcat can be gauged by the claims that 75% of US Navy victories over Japanese aircraft, over 5,000, were attributed to the type. The 'kill' ratio has been stated as 19:1. 12,274 Hellcats were made. The engine was a 2,000 hp Pratt & Whitney R-2800.

Hellcats were used in Korea, in an unusual way. Packed with explosives, and flown by remote control from accompanying aircraft, they were used as guided missiles, with some success against vital targets such as bridges.

Last of the Grumman piston fighters was the F8F Bearcat. Too late for wartime service, a much modified Bearcat holds the world speed record for piston power at 528 mph (850 kph). An interesting feature was that the wing-tips were intended to break off if overstressed. On one 11g pull-out the tips broke off as designed, so effectively easing the strain on the rest of the structure that it only needed new wing-tips before flying again.

> *Another fine Grumman naval type was the Avenger torpedo-bomber. In a US Navy night-flying exercise, an officer on the ground was charged with firing a flare if any landing aircraft had their wheels raised.*
>
> *When an Avenger belly-landed amid a shower of sparks he was so shocked about failing his duty that he accidentally fired the flare, hitting the nearby driver of a waiting jeep.*
>
> *The driver in turn was so startled he let the clutch out and knocked over the flare-holder. Despite the series of mishaps, no one was seriously hurt.*

Grumman F-14 Tomcat
potent front-line naval fighter

Grumman followed its fine piston-engine naval fighters with the 1947 jet-powered Panther, which served with distinction in Korea, and its swept-wing successor, the Cougar. The F-14, continuing the cat theme with the name Tomcat, is a twin-engine variable geometry, or 'swing-wing', fighter which first flew in 1970.

Early experience was unpromising, for it crashed on its second flight due to hydraulic problems, and in 1972 Grumman were losing so much money building the F-14 that they threatened to stop production until the price was raised. Once these problems were overcome the F-14 became the principal US Navy fighter, which it remains. Engines are two Pratt & Whitney TF30s, or in later versions General Electric F110s.

The missiles and electronics aboard enable the F-14 to shoot down an enemy aircraft over 100 miles away, provided the target really is identified as hostile at such a distance.

Grumman Gulfstreams
pride of the business fleets

Grumman became worried in the 1950s about their reliance on military business and moved more strongly into the civil field. An early venture was an unlikely one, a biplane made for crop-spraying called the Ag-Cat, which first flew in 1957, but Grumman had judged their market well and sold over 2,500.

When Grumman flew the elegant twin Rolls-Royce Dart powered Gulfstream business turboprop in 1958, many doubted whether companies would pay $750,000 for such a machine. They did, and some 200 were sold. Grumman were encouraged enough to launch a large business jet successor. The Gulfstream 2 first flew in 1966, and improved versions up to today's Gulfstream 4 have all sold well.

These jets have transatlantic range. Grumman (since 1978 this side of the business has been a separate company, Gulfstream American) have remained loyal to Rolls-Royce for their engines, mainly Speys but progressing to Tays for the latest versions.

A freak but tragic accident befell a Gulfstream pilot as he walked down the aircraft steps.
Unknowingly he had parked with the high tail touching a high-voltage cable. As he stepped on to the tarmac he completed the circuit and was killed.

Handley Page biplane airliners
sedate pioneers of air travel

Handley Page set up their own airline in 1919 using fairly crude conversions of their wartime bombers. Some versions carried two intrepid passengers in an open front cockpit, advertised as an attraction for those who preferred to travel in the open. Austere as they were, Handley Page Air Transport were the first in the world to serve meals in flight.

The improved W.8, first flown in December 1919, is widely considered the first real airliner. One served from 1922 till 1932, logging 5,000 flying hours, a modest enough figure today but an achievement in its day. At first passengers could watch the ground below (not far below then!) through portholes in the floor, but many found this unsettling and the idea was dropped.

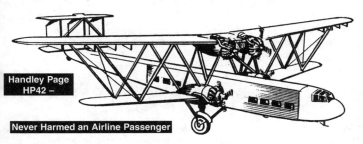

Handley Page HP42 –

Never Harmed an Airline Passenger

The greatest of the biplane airliners was the four-engine HP42, with Bristol Jupiter engines, first flown in November 1930. Only 8 were made but they epitomised the leisurely and luxurious style of Imperial Airways.

Cabins were appointed like those of ocean liners, and four-course meals were served – at 95 mph (152 kph) there was time enough to eat them. Fast they were not, but on shorter runs like London to Paris the overall journey time from checking in to leaving the destination airport was similar to that of today.

Remarkable for the time was their perfect safety record – not a single airline passenger was harmed in an HP42, even though one was lost in wartime service, and most of the rest were wrecked on the ground in gales whilst on war service. These fine aeroplanes had stirring names to match – Hannibal, Hadrian, Horsa, Hengist, Hanno, Helena, Horatio, and Heracles were fondly remembered by all who flew in them.

PIONEERING DAYS

Standards of comfort and safety in 1919 were far from those of today. Some passengers were so nervous that members of the airline staff took them to a bar to soothe their fears. Such fears were not entirely unfounded – one flight from London to Paris included 16 forced landings – all passengers bar one brave soul ended their journey by other means.

Pilots devised their own tricks for overcoming problems – one landed at Croydon in thick fog by lining up on the Crystal Palace and calculating his distance to go!

No lifejackets were carried in the early years, but it was claimed some pilots took their own.

Despite its antiquated appearance, the HP42 had a good performance even on three engines. When an engine failed, as the best-known of Imperial Airways captains, O.P. Jones, was taking off, his inexperienced co-pilot shouted "whoa," pointing at the offending engine, repeating the "whoa" when his captain remained silent.

'OP' took off and completed a circuit without a word, then turned and said "you shout whoa to a horse, not to an aeroplane."

Handley Page biplane bombers
defenders of the Empire

Frederick Handley Page ('HP') responded to an Admiralty request for a 'bloody paralyser' to halt German advances with an ambitious 100ft (31m) span bomber.

The great biplane bomber flew as the O/100 at the end of 1915, powered by two of the new Rolls-Royce Eagles. The later O/400 was an improved version.

These Handley Page biplanes pioneered strategic bombing. A dramatic tactic sometimes used was to glide in silently down to a height of 80 feet before releasing the bombs in the hope of escaping detection.

About 600 of these big bombers were built. Some were produced in America, and 'HP' was keen to fly them to Britain, an audacious idea considering no aeroplane had yet flown the Atlantic.

In post-war years O/400s made many fine long-distance flights. Such flights were still hazardous. 51 O/400s left Britain to fly to Egypt in 1919, but only 26 arrived. Navigation was still primitive too. To aid flights crossing the Middle Eastern desert, a long furrow was ploughed to mark the way.

Even mightier was the 126ft (39m) span V/1500, with four Eagle engines. Designed to reach Berlin, it was poised for its first such mission when the cease-fire was agreed. Just after peace returned, 'HP' on an impulse offered to take a party of journalists aloft in a V/1500. The 40 so carried was a record; present-day airworthy authorities would be aghast at the lack of seats in the aircraft.

A V/1500 went into action just once, to suppress a tribal rebellion in Afghanistan. It seems the arrival of the giant so cowed the rebels that they surrendered. Various updated successors to the O/400 followed throughout the 1920s, with the last Handley Page biplane bomber, the Heyford, entering service in 1933.

> *The first O/100 had to be moved at night by road from the factory to airfield with wings folded. 'HP' himself climbed trees in gardens to prune projecting branches, under aggrieved protests from householders.*

THE EAGLE SPREADS ITS WINGS

The Handley Page O/100 marked an incidental milestone in aviation history – it was the first to be powered by Rolls-Royce engines.

At the outbreak of war, Henry Royce was asked to build Renault aero-engines. He disliked their design and determined to produce his own.

By extraordinary effort he had his first Eagle engine running within six months. Most engines of the time struggled to reach their intended output, but the Eagle went on past its designed 200hp to reach 225hp on its first run.

Eagles were used in many wartime bombers and in early postwar airliners. They were exceptionally reliable but did occasionally leak water. Some prudent pilots carried chewing gum for makeshift repairs.

The greatest moments of glory for the Eagles were on the first non-stop Atlantic flight, the first flight from Britain to Australia, and most of the first to South Africa. All were in adapted Vickers Vimys.

Most Rolls-Royce piston engines were named after birds of prey, including the famous Merlin which took its name from the raptor, not the magician.

Handley Page Halifax
wartime heavy bomber

Designer George Volkert first designed a twin-engine bomber with two Rolls-Royce Vulture engines, but when this unit ran into serious problems he changed the design to take four Merlins, although the majority of later Halifaxes used Bristol Hercules engines.

First flight was on 25th October, 1939. Operations started in March 1941 with daytime raids, but the level of losses soon led to concentration on night missions. Losses remained high and it was realised that enemy action was not the sole cause.

The problem was traced to the rudder design making the aircraft uncontrollable and this was remedied. Another change was to increase the wingspan to achieve greater height.

**The Halifax –
Handley Page's Heavy
Bomber Workhorse**

The 'Hallybag' lacked the load-carrying ability of the Lancaster which handled the raids which made headlines, but it undertook a wider range of duties than its partner-in-arms. Halifaxes were used as heavy bombers, for anti-submarine work, minelaying, paratroop dropping and glider towing. It was the only tug aircraft to tow the tank-carrying Hamilcar glider. 6,176 Halifaxes were made.

Their swansong, together with a transport conversion called the Halton, came on the Berlin Airlift. The last RAF Halifax was retired in 1952. Not one was preserved, but in 1973 an almost intact example was found in a Norwegian lake. It was restored to non-flying display condition and now once more a specimen of the machine in which so many fought courageously may be seen.

> *Pilot Joe Herman's Halifax was hit over Holland on 4th November 1944. Before he could put on his parachute he found himself thrown out of the aircraft. Having fallen about 12,000 feet in the dark he hit something and grabbed it.*
>
> *The 'something' proved to be the legs of his gunner, whose parachute was just opening. Both descended on the one parachute. There have been various stories of two people sharing parachutes, but most are hard to authenticate. However, Joe Herman's miraculous experience is well documented.*

IT'S A SECRET! OR IS IT?

The very existence of the Halifax was supposed to be highly secret at the time of its first flight. During the flight, test pilot James Cordes noticed a river of which he had been unaware bordering the airfield (with which he was unfamiliar).

Then he realised the 'river' was the reflection of the sun from a long line of spectators' cars – so much for 1939 security!

Handley Page Hampden

fast but vulnerable medium bomber

German-born designer Gustav Lachmann (who was interned during the war but later allowed to resume work) produced the Hampden with a slender fuselage flown from a fighter-style cockpit.

First flown in 1936, the Hampden was fast but in war service suffered heavy losses. Sent at first on daytime operations, sometimes as many as half the force were lost. The defensive armament was too light, and a further drawback was that if the pilot was hit no-one else could take control. As if that wasn't enough, the slim fuselage and twin tail-fins led some British gunners to mistake it for the Dornier Do17.

Known as the 'Flying Suitcase', the Hampden was powered by two Bristol Pegasus engines. The similar Hereford used perpetually overheating Napier Daggers and was confined to training.

The Hampden was one of the principal RAF medium bombers until 1942, and some good results were achieved. Two VCs were awarded to Hampden crew members. The type also served well as a torpedo bomber and for minelaying.

Contemporary with the Hampden was another bomber made by Handley Page, the Harrow.

It was obsolete when it entered service, but one was involved in an unusual accident, as one of the few aeroplanes to be involved in a collision with a train!

Surprisingly, all the occupants survived after the unduly low landing approach.

Another much later collision with a train involved a helicopter in Canada. The pilot needed a place to set down and could only find a railway line. He first flew up and down the line, but just after landing a train appeared. It had been in a tunnel when the pilot flew overhead. No-one was hurt.

Handley Page Jetstream
the good design which bankrupted the company

The Jetstream is a twin-turboprop business aircraft or small airliner. Unlike most of its competitors at the time, there was enough headroom to walk in the aisle. It first flew in 1967, but although the design was sound, costs were rising and Handley Page collapsed.

Ironically, despite causing the demise of one of the great names of aviation history, the Jetstream has gone on to become a world-wide success with over 400 sold. After a complex rescue, production was restarted by Scottish Aviation, now part of British Aerospace.

The RAF helped with an order for 26 (one of which was lost after being filled with petrol instead of turbine fuel) and civil sales followed. The present version is the much improved and enlarged 29-seat Jetstream 41.

Handley Page post-war airliners
the elusive quest for success

The company were quick to re-enter the airliner business after the war, with the medium-haul Hermes powered by 4 Bristol Hercules engines. Perhaps they were too quick, for on the first flight in December 1945 the prototype crashed, killing the crew. The elevators were virtually uncontrollable – did 'HP' curtail the usual pre-first-flight taxiing trials to save time?

An enlarged Hermes entered service with BOAC in 1950, but they were withdrawn only two years later.

The economics were poor – fuel consumption was not helped by its trait of flying perpetually tail-down. Its reputation was further dented when one landed in the Sahara Desert due to a gross navigation blunder, although in this case the aeroplane was blameless.

More successful was the military version, the Hastings, which served the RAF from 1948 until 1977. It gave good service on the Berlin Airlift and generally thereafter, although its record was marred in 1965 by a fatigue failure in the elevator structure which killed 41 people, the worst RAF accident fatality toll.

In the Herald, first flown in 1955, Handley Page were one of many seeking the El Dorado of riches in replacing the thousands of Douglas DC-3s still plying the airways of the world. The company made a false start in using 4 piston engines, but seeing the proven attractions of turbine power had to lose time in adapting the Herald to take two Rolls-Royce Darts.

Most unluckily, that normally most reliable of engines suffered a major failure in the first Dart-Herald en route to the 1958 Farnborough show. One engine caught fire and fell off, and it was only by a fine piece of flying by test pilot Hedley Hazelden that the occupants were saved. The Herald finally entered service in 1962, four years after the rival Fokker F-27.

The Herald offered few real advantages – they even looked similar apart from the fin shape – and most airlines opted for the proven F-27. In 1965 came further disasters: two Heralds broke up in the air. Corrosive fluids had been collecting in the bottom of the fuselage until the structure failed. Just 48 Heralds were sold, but after the problems were sorted out they served well and some remain in service after 30 years.

Handley Page Victor
the last of the V-bombers

The Victor used an unusual crescent-shaped wing, with decreasing sweep-back towards the wing-tip. It was first flown by Hedley Hazelden in December 1952. The first prototype was later lost due to tailplane flutter. In some ways the Victor was superior to the Avro Vulcan, notably in having a longer bomb-bay with consequent ability to carry a heavier load.

Early Victors were powered by 4 Armstrong Siddeley Sapphires. The B2 version switched to the Rolls-Royce Conway, and was virtually a new aeroplane, amongst other changes having a longer span wing. Bombing missions switched to low-level in the early 1960s, and from 1965 onwards the Victor's duty changed again as most were converted to tankers, and it was in this role it spent the rest of its career.

In the Falklands conflict up to 10 Victors were needed to support each Vulcan which bombed Port Stanley – Victors refuelled each other to reach the more distant contacts. The last Victors were retired in 1993, outliving the Vulcan by ten years and becoming the last of the great V-bombers.

THE FLYING TANKERS

Refuelling in flight was developed in the 1930s, notably by Alan Cobham, who founded the company Flight Refuelling.

The technique gives almost unlimited range, but needless to say requires very precise flying.

One Victor was lost when a Buccaneer hit its tail. Even more serious was a collision involving an American tanker and bomber combination which resulted in three nuclear weapons dropping on Spain and a fourth falling into the sea.

A FEAT OF DETECTION

The loss of the first Victor B2 in the Irish Sea is an example of how painstaking accident investigation can be.

16 trawlers recovered 592,000 fragments. The cause was traced to a pitot head (a measuring point for the instruments) becoming detached and giving spurious control responses.

Hawker Hart and Fury
biplane classics

Designer Sydney Camm chose a new Rolls-Royce engine, the Kestrel, to power both his Hart light bomber and Fury fighter. Considered by many to be the most elegant of all biplanes, the Hart and Fury looked similar but were quite different aeroplanes.

The Hart first flew in 1928 and entered service in 1930. It was faster than the best RAF fighters of the time. There were many variations on the Hart theme, including the Demon two-seat fighter, Osprey naval version, and the improved Hind bomber. At one time no less than 28 RAF squadrons flew members of the Hart family, and there were several export sales. Equally importantly, the Hart ensured Hawker's survival in lean times, without which there would have been no Hurricane.

The Fury single-seat fighter entered service in 1931. It was the first RAF aircraft able to exceed 200 mph (320 kph). These lovely biplane fighters epitomised the best of pre-war RAF flying.

Hawker Hunter
outstanding jet fighter

Hawkers entered the jet age in 1947 with a fighter which was to become the naval Sea Hawk. Like most Sydney Camm designs, it was a notably elegant machine which gave good service to the Royal Navy and several overseas navies. As late as 1971 the Indian Navy was using Sea Hawks in action against Pakistan.

After flying a string of intermediate prototypes, Hawker flew the swept-wing Hunter on 20th July 1951. Some would consider the Hunter to be the finest-looking military jet ever made, its smooth sweeping lines contrasting with the purposeful brutality of the fast jets of today.

On 7th September 1953 Neville Duke set a new world speed record of 727.6 mph (1171 kph) in a red-painted Hunter with reheat on its Rolls-Royce Avon. Most Hunters used various marks of Avon but some were fitted with the Armstrong Siddeley Sapphire in case of intractable problems with the Avon.

After early problems such as engines stopping when the guns were fired, the Hunter became a world-wide success, always immensely popular with pilots. Several formation teams flew Hunters with impressive effect, one performing a 22-aircraft loop. Hunters were sold to many countries, and licence production took place in Holland and Belgium.

A major customer was Switzerland, which flew the type for 36 years, from 1958 until 1994. In its home country, Hunters served with the Royal Navy until 1995.

A supersonic successor, the P1121, was being built in 1957 and it might well have followed the success story of the Hunter. Sadly the responsible government minister made one of those decisions which almost defy belief and decided that missiles would replace all manned fighters.

The end of the P1121 ensured that the supersonic fighters which have sold around the world have been supplied by France and America instead of Britain.

Hawker Hurricane
Battle of Britain stalwart

The Hurricane may never have been as well-known to the public as its famous partner the Spitfire, but around twice as many Hurricanes as Spitfires fought in the Battle of Britain and it was one of the most vital barriers against the Nazi onslaught.

Designer Sydney Camm started working on a monoplane derived from the Fury, but before long it became an entirely new aeroplane. 8 machine-guns were to be carried (biplanes were generally armed with only two), and the new Rolls-Royce Merlin was the engine.

'George' Bulman first flew this historic fighter on 6th November 1935. Hawker directors saw the threat from Germany and ordered materials and new factory space for 1,000 Hurricanes without an order, a bold step which saved vital time.

In the Battle of Britain Hurricanes destroyed more enemy aircraft than all other fighters combined. The Hurricane was slower than a Spitfire or Messerschmitt Bf109 but it had a tight turning circle and had the important attribute of being steady when the guns were fired. It was also tough – it is believed no Hurricane ever suffered a

Hawker Hurricane
Bulwark of the Battle of Britain

structural failure other than due to enemy action, and it often returned home with damage which would have been fatal to its contemporaries.

Usual practice was for Hurricanes to engage the bombers and Spitfires the fighter escorts, but in battle matters were rarely so orderly. The sole Fighter Command VC was awarded to James Nicholson. His Hurricane was ablaze when he saw a Bf110 in front of him. He delayed baling out long enough to shoot it down.

In 1941 Hurricanes started a new career, as 'Hurribombers' armed with two bombs, cannon, and later rockets to attack ground targets. They proved most effective in this task.

Some Hurricanes served at sea. To protect convoys, a number of merchant ships were fitted with a catapult enabling a Hurricane to be launched over the bows. Some successes were achieved, notably against marauding Focke-Wulf Condors, but after the mission the pilot had to ditch and hope a ship could stop for him – an uncertain prospect in a battle. Later came the better solution of flying Sea Hurricanes from small escort carriers.

14,531 Hurricanes were built up till July 1944, when production ended in favour of the Typhoon. Nearly 3,000 were sent to Russia.

> *Design can be influenced by trivial matters. The Hurricane undercarriage could have been simpler with a wider wing centre-section, but this had been governed by the width of the doors on the assembly shop.*

Hawker Typhoon, Tempest and Sea Fury

potent low-level fighters

Hawkers conceived the Typhoon as a successor to the Hurricane, built around a 2,000 hp engine. First of the family to fly was the Tornado in 1939 with a Rolls-Royce Vulture, but both engine and aircraft were cancelled.

The Typhoon with a Napier Sabre flew in February 1940 but was soon in trouble. In May test pilot Philip Lucas nursed the prototype back after the rear fuselage started to fail, a feat for which he was awarded the George Medal.

RAF service started in September 1941 but over the next year losses were high due to failures of the rear fuselage and of the troublesome Sabre engine. Later however the Typhoon became a most effective low-level fighter and ground attack aircraft, although the Sabre remained worryingly temperamental. The chin-mounted radiator gave it a pugnacious appearance.

The Tempest had a thinner wing (the thick Typhoon wing limited high altitude performance) and entered service in April 1944. Soon its 425 mph (680 kph) speed was being used to good effect against V1 flying bombs – Tempests destroyed 638 of the missiles.

Last of the family, the Fury, flew in 1944 with a Bristol Centaurus engine and new elliptical wing. It served as the naval Sea Fury, being widely used in Korea, but land-based Furies were flown in Pakistan and Iraq. Some served in Germany until the 1970s. Modified versions are popular for racing in America.

Hawker Siddeley (now British Aerospace) Harrier

unique short take-off and vertical landing strike aircraft

Sir Sydney Camm teamed with Sir Stanley Hooker of Bristol Siddeley engines in the late 1950s to develop a vertical take-off fighter. Later the emphasis changed to short take-off to carry heavier loads. At the heart of the P1127, as it then was, was the Pegasus 'vectored thrust' turbofan.

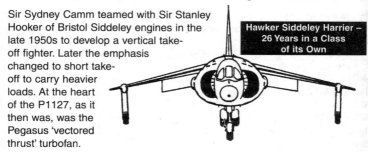

Hawker Siddeley Harrier – 26 Years in a Class of its Own

Using some ideas of a French designer, Wibault, four nozzles deflect the jet effluxes at any angle from straight rearwards to past the vertical, the 'four-poster' arrangement.

First hovering flight was on 21st October, 1960, and the critical first transition to wing-borne flight was made the following September. The test flying was dangerous, for this was an entirely new form of flight, and there were several accidents.

An early version named Kestrel was flown by a joint British, German, and American trials unit in 1964. The Kestrel was to have been followed by the supersonic P1154, but this was cancelled in favour of the subsonic Harrier strike aircraft. The Harrier entered service in 1969. At first the accident rate was high, for much was to be learned about this new type of operation.

Two Harriers were lost after their engines ran down. After justifiably ejecting the pilots learned that the engines had recovered and the Harriers had flown on for some time. The remedy was an override to the complex engine control system.

Soon the unique abilities of the Harrier were recognised by the US Marine Corps who bought 112 as the AV-8A. The USMC also exploited another feature of the Harrier, the ability to move the nozzles in flight to give stunning manoeuvrability.

Another early customer was the Spanish Navy who bought AV-8As to avoid a British arms embargo on Spain. Some wondered, would the Harrier burn the wooden deck of Spain's carrier Dedalo? It didn't.

In partnership with MacDonnell Douglas the much improved AV-8B has been developed with larger wing and more modern systems, together with the British equivalents GR5 and GR7.

The naval Sea Harrier opened up entirely new possibilities for maritime aviation. Britain built 3 special carriers for the purpose, originally called 'through-deck cruisers' to please the politicians who had decided Britain would have no more carriers. The capabilities of the Sea Harrier in carrying heavier loads were much enhanced (by about 30%) by the ingenious idea of the 'ski-jump' ramps on the bows of the ships.

In the Falklands, Sea Harriers and later RAF Harriers played such a vital part that without them the operation might not have been possible. They destroyed 22 Argentine aircraft, but much of their effort was in attacking ground targets.

In 1969 the Harrier was the first aircraft of its kind in the world. It is remarkable that 26 years later it remains the only successful aeroplane in its class.

> *Sub-Lt Ian Watson's Sea Harrier was low in fuel over the Atlantic. Spotting the Spanish freighter Alraigo he landed on top of her deck cargo of containers, despite being unable to communicate with the crew.*
>
> *The ship reached port with its unlikely cargo perched precariously on the containers.*

Hawker Siddeley (now British Aerospace) Hawk
highly successful jet trainer and strike aircraft

Best-known to the public as the mount of the renowned Red Arrows since 1980, the Hawk was designed as an advanced trainer for the RAF. First flown in 1974, and powered by a Rolls-Royce/Turbomeca Adour turbofan, the Hawk has become a world-wide export success.

A notable coup was its selection by the US Navy who fly it as the T-45A Goshawk. The Hawk has excellent handling, as demonstrated by the Red Arrows, and has a low accident rate for its class.

As happens to most trainers, armed strike versions have appeared since the early 1980s, and these again have followed the widespread sales success of the trainers.

THE NAMING GAME

Naming internationally built products can be difficult. Rolls-Royce names its jets after rivers, whereas French partner Turbomeca name theirs after Pyrranean peaks.

Adour was a neat compromise – it is a river in southern France

Even 'Concorde' was the result of long deliberation. Supposedly it resulted from scanning an English-French dictionary for words similar in both languages.

'Brutal' and 'Carnage" were naturally pssed over before reaching Concorde, or was it Concord? There was still long argument over that final 'e'.

Hawker Siddeley Nimrod
jet submarine hunter

The Nimrod, well named after 'The Mighty Hunter', first flew in 1967 and remains the RAF anti-submarine defence. The aeroplane was developed from the Comet airliner, with a new fuselage packed with electronics.

As well as its main duty, the Nimrod plays an important part in directing operations during sea rescues. To extend patrol time, two of the four Rolls-Royce Speys are shut down in cruise.

An early warning version was cancelled due to technical problems with the complex electronics and rapidly rising costs.

Heinkel He 111

a principal Luftwaffe bomber

Ernst Heinkel flew a clean-looking single-engine monoplane, his He 70, in 1932. A number were used as light airliners and bombers, and one was bought by Rolls-Royce as a flying test-bed. The He 111, which was to become notorious over Britain as a villain of the Blitz, was a larger twin-engine derivative.

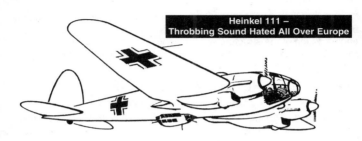

**Heinkel 111 –
Throbbing Sound Hated All Over Europe**

A few served as airliners but most had no such peaceful intent. Like most German military aeroplanes of the day, the He 111 was sent into action in the Spanish civil war, and from 1939 onwards it flew on all fronts.

Luftwaffe commanders were deceived by their experience in Spain, where the He 111 was faster than most opposing fighters and losses were light.

Battle of Britain experience showed its vulnerability to fighters unless well protected by escorts, and even then losses eventually prompted a switch to night raids. Nevertheless much damage was caused to airfields and cities. Its unsynchronised engines made a characteristic throbbing sound which came to be detested by civilians.

The He 111 served throughout the war, although by the end it was obsolete. In 1944 a few air-launched V1 flying bombs.

Over 7,300 were made, most with Junkers Jumo 211 engines. In post-war Spain it was built as the Casa 2111 until 1956, with Merlin engines.

HEINKEL'S STRANGE TWIN

An oddity was the He 111Z 'Zwilling' ('Twin'), comprising two He 111s linked together with a fifth engine in the middle.

It towed aloft the great Me 321 glider or 3 smaller gliders (a tricky undertaking!). Only a few were made.

Heinkel He 162 Salamander
'people's jet' fighter

By late 1944 matters were desperate in Germany. On 8th September 1944 a specification was issued for a 'people's fighter' (Volksjäger), to be flown by inexperienced Hitler Youth pilots.

Heinkel completed the design in 6 weeks and flew the He 162 on 6th December, an astonishing timescale. Perhaps it was too hurried, for 4 days later it broke up during a demonstration.

The He 162 had a single BMW jet engine mounted on top of the fuselage behind the pilot, who had an early ejection seat to take him clear of the engine. Much of the structure was of wood. Speed was respectable but the He 162 was demanding to fly and it was as well for the intended raw pilots that it saw little service, largely due to shortage of fuel.

Heinkel 177 Greif (Griffon)
flawed German heavy bomber

It is strange that Germany never developed a satisfactory heavy bomber. The He 177 used four engines in pairs coupled to drive single propellers, making it look like an outsize twin.

First flown in 1939, the He 177 was soon in trouble. Prototypes broke up and the complex engine arrangement was prone to catching fire, a problem never fully solved. The He 177 was used on both Western and Eastern fronts from 1942 onwards, but was unsatisfactory in service. About 900 were made.

Heinkel 178
first jet in the world to fly

Ernst Heinkel took jet engine pioneer Hans von Ohain under his wing in 1936. An engine was run in 1937, followed by the first flight of a jet-propelled aeroplane two years later. The historic first flight was handled by Erich Warsitz on 27th August 1939. The engine was a Heinkel HeS 3b unit.

Heinkel's pioneering enterprise brought little reward. Due to the politics of German military procurement, progress was slow. Heinkel flew a jet fighter, the twin-engine He 280 in 1941 but it was never ordered into production. The company had to wait until the end of 1944 before receiving orders for a jet, the He 162.

Heinkel 219 Uhu (Owl)
excellent twin-engine fighter

Another victim of German politics, the He 219, first flown in 1942, was designed to match the Mosquito. It did so, but Ernst Heinkel had his enemies and just 286 were made.

The Uhu has a place in aeronautical history as the first in service with an ejection seat. It was also the first operational German aircraft with a tricycle undercarriage.

Hughes H-4 Hercules
the largest aeroplane ever made

Howard Hughes had broken many prewar records in his H-1 racer, including the world speed record and fastest US coast-to-coast time. In 1942 he embarked on a bigger venture, his mighty 8-engine, 700 seat Hercules flying boat, dubbed the 'Spruce Goose' from its wooden structure. Its 320ft (97 m) span has never been surpassed.

By the time it was ready the war was over and there was no chance of orders, but Hughes persisted in completing it. On 2nd November 1947 Hughes, alone aboard the giant, made its one brief flight.

It has been suggested that Hughes was discouraged from making a more extensive flight, or ever flying it again, by handling problems and ominous noises from the wooden structure. He may also have become less confident after a serious crash in another aeroplane the previous year.

The Hercules is now preserved as a tourist attraction. Hughes himself became president of the airline TWA but degenerated into an eccentric recluse.

Hunting Percival (later BAC) Jet Provost
standard RAF trainer for nearly 40 years

Hunting Percival was formed in 1942 when the Hunting shipping group bought the Percival aircraft company. A piston-engine trainer was flown in 1950 and entered RAF and overseas service as the Provost.

More important was its jet successor which used Provost wings and other parts. There must have been good reserve of strength to cope with much higher speed without redesign.

The Jet Provost flew in 1954, with an Armstrong Siddeley Viper engine. The Jet Provost entered RAF service in 1955. Much was made at the time of the 'all-through' jet training, in which student pilots flew jets from the time of their first flights. Later it was found more economical to re-introduce piston-engine training for the early stages.

Later Jet Provosts had pressurised cockpits and more power, and like most initially harmless trainers a more aggressive armed version appeared, the BAC 167 Strikemaster. Many were exported.

The RAF retired its last Jet Provosts in 1994 after nearly 40 years of excellent service.

A few private pilots have bought Jet Provosts. One took his brother for a flight but after turning inverted found himself alone!

The ejection seat had not been properly secured and both seat and startled passenger parted company with the aircraft, luckily at enough height for the parachute to open.

Ilyushin Il-2 Shturmovik
most numerous of all Second World War aeroplanes

The single-engine Shturmovik (Storm) was designed for ground attack against infantry and tank formations. One of the reasons the Il-2 proved so effective was that it was designed with armour plate to protect it from ground fire at the outset, rather than added as an afterthought.

First flown in October 1940 (a close predecessor flew the previous year), at first production was slow, to Stalin's displeasure, but from 1942 until 1944 vast numbers were turned out, the total of 36,163 being the highest for any aircraft other than light aeroplanes.

It was a vital weapon in the advances of the Red Army. Stalin, recovered from his earlier anger, stated that "the Il-2 is as vital to our Red Army as air or bread."

Ilyushin Il-28
early Russian jet bomber

Ilyushin did well to fly this twin-jet in 1948, a year before the comparable Canberra. Ironically Britain had helped the Russians by supplying some Rolls-Royce Nene engines, and a version of this powerplant was used in the 5,000 or so of the bombers made.

A few were used by the Russian airline Aeroflot on mail services, perhaps qualifying it as the second jet airliner in service, but whether it counts as an 'airliner' is debatable.

Ilyushin have however made a long line of genuine airliners, from the 1946 piston-engine Il-12 and improved Il-14, often given as presents to third-world country dictators to induce them into the communist fold, to the first Russian wide-body, the 1976 Il-86 and its present-day successor the Il-96.

Junkers J 13
landmark in metal airliner design

Hugo Junkers was the pioneer of stressed-skin metal construction, flying an all-metal monoplane as early as 1915. Largely thanks to his advanced structural design, by the late 1930s Junkers was the largest aircraft builder in the world.

The J 13, later renamed F 13, was a single-engine monoplane transport with the 4 passengers seated in a closed cabin. It was clad in a corrugated metal skin, for some years a Junkers trademark (but one which caused considerable drag). First flight was in June 1919. Over 300 of these rugged machines were made.

They proved outstanding in tropical climates and outback regions where conditions were ruinous to wooden structures. They could be fitted with wheels, floats or skis. Some flew for over 20 years, unimpressive today but excellent for the time. In structural terms the J 13 is one of the most significant of all airliners.

British aircraft builder Frederick Handley Page was fond of recounting a landing accident to a G 13 on which the name JUNKERS was prominently painted.

The fuselage broke behind the letter 'K'. 'HP' would gleefully point out that the remaining part spelled 'JUNK'.

Junkers Ju 52/3m
Germany's tough airliner and military transport

The Ju 52/3m trimotor was a standard Lufthansa airliner of the late 1930s, some 200 being in use at one time, and it was flown in the thousands by the wartime Luftwaffe. A single-engine Ju 52 flew in 1930, followed by the trimotor two years later.

The Ju 52/3m was everywhere during the war, flown as a transport and for paratroop dropping. In the latter role casualties were often heavy amongst these fairly slow transports with their fixed undercarriages; in the invasion of Crete some 170 were lost. However generally the 'Tante Ju' or 'Iron Annie' was well liked by crews. The number built is uncertain but 4,835 is widely quoted.

Further numbers were made in France and Spain. Some served with post-war airlines (including BEA for a short time) but the type was obsolete by then. Others continued as military transports, probably the last being a handful with the Swiss Air Force which soldiered on until the early 1980s.

Junkers 87 Stuka
the dreaded dive-bomber

The Stuka (the name refers to all dive bombers) was hated by soldiers on the receiving end of its attentions, for when unopposed it was accurate and devastating.

Instantly recognisable by its cranked wing and fixed undercarriage, its arrival was advertised by a screaming siren fixed to the wing and intended to demoralise those below.

The Ju 87 was less successful when Allied fighters were around, for it was slow and vulnerable, so much so that its use became limited to regions where they were unlikely to be met.

The Stuka was not always accurate. John Frost, later to lead the heroic stand at Arnhem, was under severe pressure in North Africa from large German forces.

When he heard the fearsome sound of Stuka sirens he feared his end had come, until he saw all the bombs fall right on the Germans' own positions.

Junkers 88
the best wartime German bomber

The Ju 88 started its career badly, for the prototype crashed within a few days of its first flight in 1936. It soon made amends and won an evaluation against its competitors. The Ju 88 was fast and versatile, being used for conventional and dive bombing, nightfighting, reconnaissance, torpedo bombing, and even as an unmanned flying bomb (see Focke-Wulf 190).

The Allies regarded the Ju 88 as the best of German bombers, but even so losses were heavy under determined fighter attacks. A problem in countering the Ju 88 was that it could be mistaken for a Blenheim. Two were landed in Britain, one by a defecting crew and the other due to a navigation error, helping to evaluate its strengths and weaknesses, and even more importantly the electronics they carried.

14,980 were built, by far the highest total for any German bomber. The engines were usually two Junkers Jumo 211s.

MURDEROUS MUSIC

Ju 88 nightfighters were armed with upward-firing cannon, called 'Schräger Musik' ('Jazz'). These enabled the fighter to attack bombers unseen from below.

It sounds impractical but it was effective, and for some time Allied bomber crews were unaware of the reason for their losses from these weapons.

Learjets
best-selling business jets

Prolific inventor William Lear, with interests ranging from autopilots to steam cars, launched the Learjet family in 1963. The first design originated in Switzerland, oddly enough based on work for a jet fighter.

The first Learjets were delivered in 1964, just over a year after the first flight. Bill Lear retired in 1969 but he judged his market well, for over 1,700 Learjets of different models have been sold. The company is now owned by Bombardier.

Lockheed C-5A Galaxy
giant freighter and first 'wide-body'

By some yardsticks the largest aircraft in the world, the C-5A can carry outsize military loads like tanks or helicopters. First flown in 1968, only 81 were built but they have been invaluable in moving military forces quickly to trouble-spots anywhere in the world.

Their ability to fly forces in this way has allowed America to cut its military presence abroad. The history of the C-5A has been far from trouble-free, for the wings have needed rebuilding and a crash during the US evacuation of Vietnam killed a tragic number of refugee children.

The engines are 4 General Electric TF39s of (now) 53,000lb thrust. These were the first 'large-fan' engines and led the way to the revolution in air travel economics from the wide-body airliners.

Indeed when the C-5A was selected over a competing design from Boeing, that company used the work on their losing submission to launch the Boeing 747 jumbo jet. Perhaps Boeing were not the losers after all.

Lockheed C-130 Hercules
workhorse to the world

Few aircraft have proved so versatile or become used so widely around the world. Wherever there are natural or man-made disasters, when relief comes it will surely arrive in the cavernous holds of the ubiquitous Hercules.

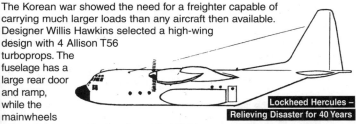

The Korean war showed the need for a freighter capable of carrying much larger loads than any aircraft then available. Designer Willis Hawkins selected a high-wing design with 4 Allison T56 turboprops. The fuselage has a large rear door and ramp, while the mainwheels

Lockheed Hercules – Relieving Disaster for 40 Years

stow in fairings on the fuselage. First flight was on 23rd August 1954.

Performance was well above specification, a rare event in the aeronautical world! Besides its task of carrying military cargo, 'Charlie 130s' (or in the RAF 'Fat Alberts') have been used for commercial freighting, as 'gunships' with sideways-pointing guns (some with whopping 105mm guns), for electronics eavesdropping and for landing and picking up special forces behind enemy lines.

Trials were even made of flying from the aircraft carrier 'Forrestal' in 1963. As well as all this, countless thousands have been saved by the part played by the C-130 in humanitarian relief, thanks to its large load capacity and ability to fly from rough strips.

At the time of writing 66 countries have bought over 2,000 Hercules. The production run of 40 years is a record for any Western aeroplane. Will it reach 50 years? It may well do so, for Lockheed are making the much improved C-130J which should take it into the next century.

THE ENTEBBE RESCUE

A spectacular mission was the rescue of hostages from a hijacked airliner by Israeli forces in 1976. 245 commandos were flown in 3 Hercules, taking the Ugandan defenders at Entebbe airport by surprise and extracting all the hostages, although marred by the death of the Israeli commander.

> *In the Gulf War special C-130 versions were used for radio jamming. Whenever Iraqi forces tried to listen to their radios they were blasted with 'heavy metal' music – one of the few times the Iraqis may have attracted sympathy?*

Lockheed Constellation

Lockheed's lovely classic piston airliner

Considered by many to be the most beautiful of piston-engine airliners, the 'Connie' was easily recognisable by its sinuously curved fuselage and small triple fins. First flight was on 9th January 1943 as a military C-69.

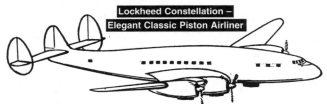

Lockheed Constellation – Elegant Classic Piston Airliner

Early examples off the line were austere wartime transports, but when peace came Lockheed were permitted to sell to the airlines. The 60 passenger Constellation entered airline service in 1946. It was pressurised, unlike the competing Douglas DC-4, and became popular with travellers.

Fairly severe technical problems early on were ironed out and Lockheed steadily improved the airliner. Engines were Wright R-3350 Cyclones. The subtle fuselage shape was harder to lengthen than the cylindrical Douglases, but Lockheed managed to add 18ft (5.5m) to produce the Super Constellation of 1950, seating up to 109.

The L-1049G version with tip-tanks could manage an Atlantic crossing in most wind conditions. Last of the line was the L-1649 Starliner of 1956, with a new wing and longer range, allowing numbing flights of 17 hours.

The jet age was nearing and only 43 Starliners were sold, bringing the total for the Constellation family to 856.

TURN UP AND FLY

In 1961 Eastern Airlines used Super Constellations displaced by jets to start the first air shuttle service, whereby travellers turned up at the airport without reservations.

A back-up aircraft was guaranteed if the scheduled flight was full, and the airline made much of well-publicised instances of the reserve aircraft taking just one passenger. Shuttles have since been introduced on other busy routes throughout the world.

Lockheed 10 Electra and family
Lockheed's heavenly twins

First flown in February 1934, the Electra was the start of one of the finest series of pre-war airliners. They were twin-engine metal monoplanes with distinctive twin tail fins. The Electra carried 10 passengers on the power of two Pratt & Whitney Wasp Juniors.

149 were made, some being used for record long-distance flights; it was in one such that Amelia Earheart disappeared in 1937. One Electra was tested in 1937 with a pioneering pressure cabin. Above all, it was the Electra which saved Lockheed from bankruptcy, allowing it to become one of the giants of aviation.

The 1937 L-14 was an enlarged 14-seat version. Several were used by the pre-war British Airways, one of which carried Neville Chamberlain to his Munich meeting with Hitler in 1938. Another was used by Howard Hughes to set a round-the-world record in an astonishing 3 days 17 hours (these airliners were the fastest of their day).

The L-18 Lodestar was a further enlargement taking, as might be guessed, 18 passengers. 625 were built, wartime BOAC flying no less than 38. The Hudson, Ventura, and Harpoon were military versions of various members of the Lockheed twins.

The Hudson was developed from the L-14 at Britain's request, and proved a most effective maritime patrol aircraft. One Hudson crew even induced a U-boat crew to surrender their vessel intact (It later served in the Royal Navy as HMS Graph, the name reflecting the mass of evaluations done on the submarine). 2,941 Hudsons were made.

> The Hudson showed its fine flying qualities when an RAF pilot misjudged his height and hit the sea – a mishap almost invariably resulting in loss of the aircraft, but the Hudson climbed away to safety.

Lockheed Electra (postwar) and Orion
turboprop airliner and its anti-submarine cousin

The Electra was a 100-seat airliner with 4 Allison 501 turboprop engines, inspired by the success of the Vickers Viscount. It first flew in 1957 and entered service the next year, too close to the jet age for healthy sales.

Two fatal structural failures due to a resonance between the engine nacelles and wings further damaged its prospects. Another accident caused by multiple engine failures after flying through a flock of starlings led to a change in engine speed on take-off; the sound supposedly resembled starling mating calls.

Only 161 Electras were sold, but all was not lost for derived from the airframe was the successful Orion anti-submarine aircraft. Around 750 are flying, including some made in Japan, and while none are being made at the time of writing it is still being actively promoted.

Lockheed P-38 Lightning

master of the Pacific air war

The unusual twin-engine twin boom P-38 was fast, had long range and was well armed. It proved highly effective in the Pacific, but less so in Europe where its lower manoeuvrability than single-engine fighters was a handicap.

The P-38 had many innovative features including a then new tricycle undercarriage and exhaust turbo-supercharging on the Allison V-1710 engines. First flight was in January 1939, and just a fortnight later it set a coast-to-coast record of 7 hours 2 minutes, an achievement marred by crashing on landing.

The aeroplane was ordered into large-scale production, and was the only US fighter made throughout America's part in the war. The RAF rejected the P-38, but not before christening it Lightning, a name later adopted in America. The poor showing in RAF testing was largely due to the American government refusing to supply the superchargers in case they fell into German hands.

In the Pacific however the P-38 reigned supreme and is believed responsible for destroying more Japanese aircraft than any other type. The 3 top-scoring American 'aces' all flew Lightnings. Another famous aviator who scored one victory was Charles Lindbergh, although he was not supposed to fly in combat.

A coup by P-38s was the interception of the aircraft carrying Admiral Yamamoto, thanks to a code-breaking success. 10,037 Lightnings were built. Some sources quote slightly less.

Lockheed P-80 (later F-80) Shooting Star

first American operational jet

Designer 'Kelly' Johnson and team produced the prototype in a remarkable 143 days after award of the contract. The effort was to some extent in vain as the engine was wrecked during ground running, delaying the first flight by 6 months until 8th January 1944. On its second flight 500 mph (800 kph) was exceeded, the first time this speed had been seen in America.

A few reached Europe before the end of the war, but saw no action. However in Korea it was heavily involved and performed with credit, although by then outclassed by swept-wing MiG-15s. 1,732 were built, mostly with Allison or General Electric J33s.

Even more successful was its trainer version, the T-33 'T-Bird', 5,819 of which were made by Lockheed and Kawasaki in Japan. Another 576 were made as Canadair Silver Stars in Canada, with Rolls-Royce Nene engines.

It is an indication of the flying qualities of these trainers that the USAF was still flying the T-33 until 1988.

Lockheed F-104 Starfighter

'the missile with a man in it'

No other aeroplane looked like the F-104: a great cylindrical fuselage was supported by tiny straight wings only 4 inches (10 cm) thick. It could fly at Mach 2 but it lacked manoeuvrability due to the small wings.

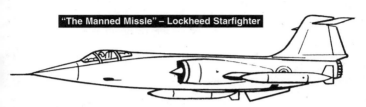

"The Manned Missle" – Lockheed Starfighter

First flight was in 1954. The engine on production aircraft was the General Electric J79 turbojet. Early versions had downward-ejecting seats, not a popular point with pilots (the high tail was a problem for upward ejection). 2,583 were made in 7 countries.

Most controversial were F-104G versions flown in Germany, where high accident rates caused a political scandal. In one year losses exceeded one per thousand hours, as much due to inexperience of high-performance jets by German air and ground crews as to faults in the aircraft – in other countries losses were modest.

In Germany the fatality rate at least was much reduced by fitting Martin-Baker seats in 1967.

Lockheed F-117A 'Stealth'

the elusive attacker

The F-117A was designed to be almost undetectable by radar. The structure shape, engine intakes and jetpipes, and use of radar absorbent coatings all play their part in this aim.

The F-117A is intended for ground attack, and has proved its worth in action, first in Panama in 1989 and again in Iraq in 1991. In this action 42 aircraft flew 1,200 missions, accurately hitting the most crucial targets, although one building full of civilians was also hit, probably due to faulty intelligence.

Because the entire design is centred around minimising the radar 'signature', performance is quite low by modern standards.

The F-117A is subsonic. Its two GE F404 engines use no afterburners as that means of thrust boosting would be too easily detected.

Lockheed P2V Neptune
guardian of the seas

First flown in 1945, the twin-engine Neptune was the principal Western anti-submarine aeroplane for much of the Cold War period. Neptunes were renowned (or infamous to their crews) for long endurance, 24 hour patrols being well within their capability. In 1946 one set a long-distance record of 11,236 miles (18,080 km) in a 55 hour flight.

Power was provided by two Wright R-3350 Cyclones, but with the tendency of military men to pack ever more equipment on board, later versions also had two Westinghouse J34 jets for boost. 1,181 Neptunes were made including some in Japan where the last came off the line in 1979. A few are still flying in 1995.

> *A Neptune crew returning to base found it closed due to weather. On enquiring about their options, they were asked by ground control how many hours fuel they had aboard.*
>
> *After replying that they had 26 hours left, they heard ground control cheerfully instruct "call us about this time tomorrow!"*

SAFETY STATISTICS

Fast combat jets suffer higher accident rates than aeroplanes on more sedate duties. Attrition rates are typically around one per 10,000 hours, but there is huge variation. Pilot losses are much lower, thanks to ejection seats.

By contrast, airline travel is astonishingly safe. Leading airlines achieve in the order of a million flights per fatal accident.

Lockheed Tristar
the last Lockheed airliner

The Tristar was Lockheed's first and last jet airliner. It is a 'wide-body' with 3 engines, two mounted under the wing and the third in the tail. All 3 large aero-engine makers bid hard for the Tristar propulsion, and the Rolls-Royce RB211 was chosen by the launch airlines.

Later it was seen that Rolls-Royce had been too optimistic in their bidding, but they really had to take some risk to remain a supplier to major airlines. The company were also unlucky to lose their Chief Designer, Adrian Lombard, at a critical stage of the engine's development.

First flight was at sunrise on 16th November 1970, the time of day giving a clue that all was not well. The engines were below the promised power, and the early start was to catch the cooler temperatures when all engines perform better.

Soon afterwards problems with the RB211 drove Rolls-Royce into receivership. The future of the Tristar and even Lockheed itself looked dubious. Both engine and airliner just survived and entered service in 1972.

After the early problems the combination of Tristar and RB211 settled down well. Because of the early problems, Lockheed were unable to build a long-range version as quickly at MacDonnell-Douglas with their rival DC-10. For a time Lockheed lost sales as a result, but regained the advantage when the reputation of the DC-10 was tarnished by two major accidents.

The Tristar gained several more important orders, including a small but prestige purchase by Pan American, but it was a temporary reprieve and sluggish sales in the first years of the 1980s induced Lockheed the end production and concentrate on military work. So ended 50 years of Lockheed airliner design.

THE LOCKHEED SCANDAL

Lockheed had long been known for forceful salesmanship, but rumours persisted that more disreputable methods had been used to secure F-104 and Tristar contracts.

The rumours turned out to be all too true and it became clear that bribery had been used on a massive scale. Lockheed evidently believed in going to the top, for even royalty and prime ministers enjoyed the company's 'hospitality'.

Most notorious recipient was Kakuei Tanaka, former prime minister of Japan, who received the equivalent of £1.4 million to influence All Nippon Airways to buy Tristars.

RB211 – FROM TEARS TO TRIUMPH

The RB211 was vital to Rolls-Royce: the company just had to be aboard the wide-body airliners to stay in the top league.

The 3-shaft design promised high efficiency, and daringly the large fan blades at the front of the engine were designed in a carbon-fibre material called Hyfil. Wisely a back-up design was developed in case of problems with Hyfil, and equally prudently Hyfil blades were flown in airline service on a few engines fitted to VC10 airliners.

These trials revealed difficulties and after great expense Hyfil was abandoned, but other problems remained and in 1971 the company was placed into receivership.

Rolls-Royce engineers have a history of plucking victory from disaster and in due course turned the RB211 into one of the most reliable engines ever made.

In the Boeing 757 the RB211-535 far outsells its American competitor, even to US airlines. The ugly duckling has truly become a swan and the latest version, the mighty Trent, with double the power of early RB211s, looks set to reap further success throughout the world.

Lockheed U-2 and SR-71 Blackbird
high-flying spies in the sky

The U-2, looking like an outsize sailplane with its 80ft (24m) span wing, flew in 1955. It was a product of the 'Skunk Works', part of Lockheed where projects were conceived in great secrecy. It was announced that the U-2 was to conduct atmospheric research, but why did that task need such secrecy?

In the summer of 1960 all was revealed. The Soviet Union announced that an aircraft violating its airspace had been destroyed. The USAF declared that it was a weather flight which had strayed, but only then did the Russians reveal that the pilot was in their hands and that cameras in the wreckage were full of film showing airfields and military sites.

The 'spy plane affair' virtually wrecked a planned summit meeting between the superpowers. The pilot, Francis Gary Powers, was later exchanged for a Soviet spy and finally killed in a helicopter accident.

For 4 years the 'overflights' had been made at 85,000ft (26,000m), above the reach of Russian defences, or so it was thought. Events proved otherwise. The U-2 had not yet outlived its usefulness, for it made flights over China and Cuba, in the latter case spotting Russian missiles arriving in 1962 and leading to American action to remove them via a naval blockade.

One mystery about the overflights is why for that of all missions a single-engine aeroplane was designed.

The U-2's successor *was* endowed with two engines. The mighty SR- 71 was one of the most impressive aircraft ever to fly. Another 'Skunk Works' project by 'Kelly' Johnson, it first flew in 1964 (as the A-11) and was capable of long flights at Mach 3. To cope with the skin heating at such speed, it was built of titanium, and even minor components required features like gold-plating of cables because of the temperatures.

A New York to London time of 1 hour 55 minutes was one demonstration of what it could do.

Crews were specially selected and even the fuel was unique to the 'Blackbird'. Actually they were coated in dark blue heat – absorbent paint. The fuselage was shaped to minimise its radar 'signature', pioneering the 'stealth' technology of today. The airframe soaked up so much heat at cruising speed that it could not be touched for half an hour after landing.

The SR-71s no longer fly – satellites do the job now, but some may be put back into service.

Lockheed Vega
the first Lockheed stars

An anomaly of the alphabetical order of this book is that the first of the long line of Lockheed aeroplanes named after celestial objects appears as their last entry. The Vega was a single-engine 4-passenger transport with a high cantilever wing. The engine was a Wright Whirlwind.

The designer was Jack Northrop, who was responsible for many fine Lockheed and Douglas types, later forming his own company. Today the Lockheed and Northrop companies are two of the industry 'giants'.

The Vega first flew in 1927 and the 128 built set a remarkable series of records. The first Vega disappeared during a race to Hawaii, but successful flights included two round-the-world records by one-eyed Wiley Post (the second time solo), several Arctic and Antarctic flights by polar explorer Sir Hubert Wilkins, records by Amelia Earheart and by another woman pilot Ruth Nichols, including one for height on diesel power, 19,928ft (6,074 m) with a Packard engine.

Lockheed switched to low-wing layouts after the Vega, with the Sirius, used by Charles Lindbergh for a flight to China, the similar Altair with retractable undercarriage and Orion airliner.

> *Sir Hubert Wilkins named Antarctic features he discovered 'Lockheed Mountains', 'Cape Northrop', and 'Whirlwind Glacier'.*

Martin B-26 Marauder

fast medium bomber

Glenn Martin had designed a range of fast bombers before World War Two. The B-10 of 1932 exceeded 200 mph, faster than any American fighter than in service.

Two early wartime types, the Maryland and Baltimore, served with the RAF and the Royal Navy as well as with the USAAF.

The Marauder was a fast twin-engine bomber with tricycle undercarriage. To start with it had a bad reputation, being thought 'hot' to handle and earning the unwelcome name of 'Widow-maker'. Once pilots mastered its handling it became one of the most effective bombers of its weight with combat losses well below the average of other types.

After the war Martin built the Canberra as the B-57, but then concentrated on missiles. The firm merged with Lockheed in 1994.

FLYING BY NUMBERS

There were two B-26s, the Marauder and the Douglas Invader. American Air Force numbering (let's not go into the US Navy system now!) was quite simple: B-26 is their 26th bomber in service, F-80 is the 80th fighter, C-47 the 47th transport (cargo) and so on. However fighters were originally P for pursuit, and light bombers A for attack.

The Douglas Invader started as the A-26, but when the A was dropped after the war the number B-26 was resurrected for it, there being no risk of confusion as the Marauder was then no longer in service. Latterly the system has been complicated by starting some sequences again from one for more recent types.

Martin flying-boats
from biplanes to great jet flying-boats

Martin started a long line of marine aircraft in 1930. Five years later came the graceful 4-engine M-130, the first truly long-range airliner. Only 3 were built but they brought new standards to long-distance flying.

They were often called the 'China Clippers' after the name of the first of the three. In World War Two and Korea, the gull-winged twin-engine Mariner flying-boats performed vital but unglamorous work in protecting Allied convoys.

The most impressive of all Martin aeroplanes, although one never to see service, was the P6M 4-jet Seamaster of 1955. Unique as a large jet-powered flying-boat, the Seamaster was intended for minelaying or reconnaissance, but only 11 were built – flight refuelling had given land-based aircraft virtually unlimited range, and jet engines do not take kindly to salt spray.

McDonnell F-4 Phantom
'Mac's Most', McDonnell's record-breaker

The Phantom (originally Phantom II – an earlier Phantom of 1945 had been the first carrier-borne jet in service) is a large twin-engine fighter designed for carrier operations. First flight was on 27th May 1958.

MacDonnell F-4 Phantom –

a Potent American Fighter

Soon records started tumbling, and it is claimed that more records fell to the type than any other aeroplane in history. Included was a world speed record of 1606 mph (2585 kph) by Lt-col Robinson in 1961, and a 10,000 mile (16,095km) flight in 18 hours with flight refuelling.

Unusually, this fighter designed for the US Navy was also widely adopted by the USAF, and subsequently by many other countries. The Royal Navy ordered Phantoms with Rolls-Royce Spey turbofans instead of the standard General Electric J79 turbojets, but these were transferred to the RAF when Britain scrapped its carriers. The Phantom was operated in Britain from 1968 until 1994.

The F-4 had excellent handling for landing on a carrier but was sensitive to handling on launch. For this reason and to overcome poor stall qualities which had caused losses in Vietnam, later aircraft had a revised wing with large leading-edge slats.

Despite such problems, it was the most important American combat aeroplane in Vietnam. 5,057 Phantoms were made.

They were still in action in 1991 in the Gulf, as 'Wild Weasels' destroying the Iraqi air defence by homing in on their radar.

> *The Israeli air force used the Phantom with great effect against their belligerent neighbours.*
>
> *One camera-gun sequence of pictures shows an Egyptian pilot ejecting – before his aircraft had been hit!*

McDonnell-Douglas airliners – see Douglas jetliners.

McDonnell-Douglas F-15 Eagle
America's front-line fighter

The F-15, which first flew in July 1972, is a large twin-engine fighter designed to meet the threat of high-performance combat aircraft appearing in the Soviet Union at the time.

Although conceived as an air superiority fighter, as usually happens later versions have been festooned with bombs and the electronics to deliver them. In this capacity F-15s destroyed a number of Iraqi Scud missile launchers in 1991.

Engines in the F-15 are Pratt & Whitney F100s, designed for this aeroplane.

Early F-15s were single-seaters, but more complex electronic systems have latterly caused a second crew member to be added.

Export sales have been made to Israel, Saudi Arabia and Japan.

McDonnell-Douglas F-18/A-18 Hornet
powerful carrier or land-based fighter

The F-18 has a strange history, for it was derived from a design by rivals Northrop. The Northrop YF-17 Cobra flew in 1974 but was not selected for production by the USAF. Northrop then teamed with McDonnell-Douglas to submit the similar but larger F-18 to the US Navy, and this time it was selected.

The agreement was that McDonnell-Douglas would be the project leader for the Navy programme, but Northrop would play a larger part for land-based export aircraft. The friends fell out when the former promoted virtually the naval F-18 for export. A lengthy and expensive lawsuit followed.

Whatever its past, the Hornet is a most effective fighter or ground attack aeroplane (hence the A-18 label). Some 1,200 have been built to date, and it has been exported to 7 countries.

McDonnell-Douglas helicopters
among the world's most advanced helicopters

McDonnell dabbled with helicopters in the 1940s, then left rotary wings alone for nearly 30 years. They returned to the field with the menacing AH-64 Apache battlefield helicopter, first flown in 1975.

This design had originated with the Hughes company, which merged with McDonnell-Douglas in 1984. The Apache has been in action in Iraq and Somalia. It has been chosen by the British army, for whom it will be made by Westland.

The more peaceful Explorer 8-seat transport, which entered service in 1995, is a world leader in 'NOTAR' (NO TAil Rotor) technology. 'Jet thrusters' linked to the rudder pedals prevent the machine spinning round. It is quiet and safer, by eliminating the risk of tail rotor failure and also the danger of personnel walking into a tail rotor.

Messerschmitt Bf109
Germany's principal wartime fighter

The Bf109 (the initials in the type number come from Willy Messerschmitt's company, Bayerische Flugzeugwerke – Bavarian Aircraft Factory) first flew in 1935 on the power of a Rolls-Royce Kestrel engine. The date and even the month of the first flight is uncertain.

Performance was good, but Messerschmitt had underestimated the need for firepower and fitted only two guns initially, compared with 8 in the new British fighters. In 1937 Bf109s were already in action in that testing-ground for German weapons and tactics, the Spanish civil war. German pilots gained vital experience, particularly in tactics. More guns were fitted after these early actions.

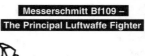

**Messerschmitt Bf109 –
The Principal Luftwaffe Fighter**

Most of the 109s in the Battle of Britain were the Bf109E ('Emil') version with Daimler-Benz DB601 engines of 1,150 hp and usually 4 guns, two cannon and two machine-guns. The Bf109E proved a formidable adversary for the RAF, particularly when flown by pilots combat-hardened in Spain.

To some extent the German advantage of experience was offset by Luftwaffe commander Hermann Goering's mishandling of the fighters by ordering them to fly in close escort to the bombers instead of letting them use their full performance.

The Bf109 remained in production throughout the war, being continually improved. The exact number made is unknown but believed to be between 31,000 and 34,000. Some were built post-war in Czechoslovakia and Spain, most of the latter powered by Merlin engines. Thus Germany's most important fighter started and ended life under Rolls-Royce power.

WHICH WAS BETTER, SPITFIRE OR BF109?

This question has been hotly debated, not least by wartime pilots. Both were continually developed so the matter is complicated by which versions to compare.

In terms of speed there was generally little to choose, but the Spitfire had the crucial advantage of a tighter turning circle. Against this, in the early days a Bf109 could escape by entering a sudden dive – its direct injection engine kept under power whilst the carburettor-fed Merlin cut briefly, until this problem was solved.

The Bf109 was less strong and some structural failures occurred, inhibiting pilots from stressing them to their limits.

Both suffered landing accidents due to their narrow undercarriages, but the Bf109 was worse in this respect, and both were limited on range when escorting bombers (since they were designed as interceptors).

On balance, the advantage generally lay with the Spitfire.

The engine of the Bf109 was 'inverted' – with the cylinders at the bottom. Rolls-Royce studied this arrangement for the Merlin but concluded that the drawbacks outweighed any advantage.

During a visit by German dignitaries to Rolls-Royce in the 1930s, a mock-up inverted Merlin was visible through a door left open, deliberately or otherwise.

Did German designers copy the idea from that glimpse through an open door?

Messerschmitt Bf110
fast twin-engine fighter of mixed fortune

Luftwaffe commander Hermann Goering held great hopes for the fast and heavily armed Bf110, and called it Zerstörer – Destroyer – in expectation of mighty victories. It was certainly fast, for it was powered by two of the same engines as used in the Bf109, but it lacked the agility of Hurricanes and Spitfires which inflicted severe losses on the Bf110 squadrons.

Later the Bf110 proved more successful as a fighter-bomber and even more so as a night-fighter. At first little success was achieved at night due to lack of airborne radar, but once this was available Bf110s caused serious losses among Allied bombers.

A planned successor, the Me 210 (the company traded under the Messerschmitt name after 1938 and the Bf prefix gave way to Me) was a failure – its handling was so bad it was scrapped.

So serious was the fiasco that Willy Messerschmitt was relieved of control of his company. A redesign as the Me 410 Hornisse finally proved reasonably successful.

Messerschmitt Me 163 Komet
dramatic and dangerous rocket fighter

One of the most remarkable aeroplanes of World War Two, the Me 163 is the only rocket-propelled fighter ever to have entered service. It was not a Messerschmitt design, but originated from tail-less protagonist Alexander Lippisch.

Lippisch designed a series of rocket-powered research aircraft in the 1930s, culminating in the Me 163B operational fighter with 660lb thrust (300 kg) Walter rocket motor. The aeroplane was a compact swept-wing tail-less design. Take-off was on a wheeled dolly which was dropped once airborne, but not too low for one pilot was killed after the wheels bounced up and hit the aircraft.

Landing was on a skid, and this was the tricky bit, for by then the Me 163 was a very fast glider and the pilot had only one try at touching down safely.

Performance was spectacular: the 600 mph (960 kph) speed was far ahead of anything else flying at the time, but this was not the advantage it seemed because the pilot closed upon the bombers so fast that he had only seconds to aim. Furthermore the fuel gave only a few minutes of combat flying, after which the powerless Me 163 was vulnerable to Allied fighters waiting near the airfield.

The Me 163 served from mid-1944 till March 1945, when it was withdrawn due to a combination of fuel shortage and its limited success. About 15-20 bombers fell prey to the Me 163, but a similar number of the rocket fighters were lost in action or from accidents.

The beast was truly dangerous, for any accidental mixing of the two fuels resulted in instant obliteration of anything and anyone around. One ground crewman blew himself to pieces by putting one of the fuels in the wrong tank.

An even more grisly fate befell pilots who overturned on landing, for the rocket fuels dissolved any organic matter (including human beings) in seconds.

The Me 163 pilots (perhaps unknowingly) fought for a tyranny, but they were among the bravest in the story of flying.

STRANGE WEAPON

Because of the difficulty in aiming the Me 163's guns in the few seconds usually available, some bizarre weapons were tried.

One was a battery of rockets pointing *upwards*, fired by a photoelectric cell activated when a bomber passed overhead.

It sounds impractical, but it is claimed one Me 163 scored a victory with this armament, despite the pilot being under orders not to engage in combat at the time.

Messerschmitt Me 262 Schwalbe

pioneering jet fighter

The Me 262 was in many ways years ahead of its time with its swept wings and technically advanced engines. The aeroplane was designed around two Junkers Jumo 004 engines mounted under the wings.

German engineers opted for efficient but technically difficult axial-flow jets, unlike most British pioneers who chose the simpler centrifugal type.

The Me 262 reached speeds of 530 mph (850 kph), some 100 mph (160kph) faster than the first Meteors, but at the cost of poor reliability and a high accident rate.

The aircraft was ready for flight by April 1941 but the engines were not, so a piston engine was fitted for early handling flights. Later two BMW engines were fitted, the Junkers units still not being available, but the piston engine was retained. This was just as well, for on the first flight so powered both BMW engines failed and the pilot was hard pressed to complete a circuit. The Me 262 flew solely under jet power in July 1942.

Entry into service was delayed until July 1944, partly because of problems with the engine programme but also because Hitler diverted effort into developing the Me 262 as a bomber.

Historians argue as to whether the Me 262 or Gloster Meteor was the first jet in service, with the majority favouring the latter. Despite poor engine reliability and other problems caused by rushing a rather undeveloped aeroplane into service, Me 262s flown by élite units scored considerable success against Allied bombers.

Other Me 262s served as fighter-bombers or night-fighters. 1,433 were built but by no means all entered service.

Messerschmitt Me 321 and 323 Gigants
the ungainly giants

The Me 321 was an enormous glider intended to carry troops and heavy loads such as tanks during the planned invasion of Britain. It was usually towed aloft by three Bf 110s, a most hazardous procedure at the best of times, let alone above a battlefield. For good measure rockets were added for take-off.

The risks became all too clear when 129 men were killed in the glider and tugs on a test flight, the worst air disaster in the world at the time.

The Me 321 would have been too late for its original purpose (first flight was in 1941), and once its impracticality was clear the design was converted to a powered version, the Me 323, at first with four engines and later with six. Some 150 of these giants were made, including some converted from the gliders, but its slow speed and great size – the span was 181ft (56 m) – made it an easy target for Allied fighters.

On one operation 23 out of 25 were shot down. That could not go on, and the Me 323 was withdrawn in 1944, no doubt to the relief of its crews and prospective passengers.

A LEGENDARY LADY

Among those who flew the Me 321 was the famous woman test pilot Hanna Reitsch. A pre-war glider pilot, the tiny 5ft. (1.5m) tall Reitsch tested many of Germany's most radical aircraft.

This remarkable woman demonstrated one of the first helicopters *inside* a large hall in 1938, and later tested the Me 321, the Me 163 rocket fighter, and a manned trials version of the VI missile. In the last days of the war she flew a daring mission into Berlin under continuous Russian fire.

She was badly injured flying an unpowered prototype of the Me 163. In a rare lapse, she had failed to strap in properly and hit her face on the pointlessly deployed gunsight. She just missed the fatal Me 321 flight referred to above, the captain forcing her out of the aircraft. Did he have foreboding about that test?

MiG (Mikoyan-Gurevich)-15
the Russian jet which shook the West

Many Western observers had regarded the Soviet Union as a backwater in aircraft design. That illusion was shattered when the swept-wing MiG-15 appeared at a display in 1948 (it had flown in February of the previous year). The shock was even greater when the MiG-15 was pitted against American and British fighters in Korea.

At first it was more than a match for its Western opponents, until the swept-wing North American Sabre arrived and redressed the balance.

The Klimov VK-1 engine was developed from the Rolls-Royce Nene after a batch of these engines was supplied by the British government to Russia. The MiG-15 was widely used and built throughout the Eastern Bloc, as well as by North Korea.

The MiG-17 looked similar but had a new wing giving better high-speed handling. Like its predecessor it was a standard type in Communist countries, including China.

Egypt used the type in the 1967 six-day war with Israel, losing most of its force on the ground to Israeli precision attacks.

> *The Egyptian MiG-17 force was largely wiped out on the ground in the 1967 6-day war, but Israeli pilots left untouched decoy aeroplanes scattered over the airfields.*
>
> *So how did the Israelis spot the fakes? The answer was they left alone those without blackening around the jet-pipes or on the ground. Smart!*

MiG-19
first Russian supersonic fighter

The MiG-19 (dubbed 'Farmer' by NATO) was the first Russian, and indeed first European, production aeroplane capable of supersonic speed in level flight. First flown in 1953, it was distantly derived from the MiG-17, but was larger and twin-engined. Many thousands were made in Russia, China, and Czechoslovakia.

The MiG family has continued to provide much of the combat aircraft strength of what was the Communist world. Some independent countries such as India have also chosen MiGs.

Later MiGs include the MiG-21 'Fishbed', the variable-sweep MiG-23 'Flogger', the fast high-flying MiG-25 'Foxbat', and the MiG-29 and 33 tactical fighters with state-of-the-art 'fly-by-wire' electronic control.

HOW HAVE MiGs COMPARED WITH WESTERN TYPES?

For a long time Western commentators regarded Russian combat aeroplanes as crude affairs. This changed in Korea, and again in Vietnam where their handling in combat was often decisively better than their American opponents which had been designed for speed at the expense of other qualities.

Generally MiG airframes have shaped up well against Western designs, but Russian engines and the vital electronics have lagged behind.

Miles light aeroplanes

fine family of sleek racers and trainers

Surprising as it may seem today, Britain was once a world leader in light aircraft building, and amongst the best were the efficient monoplanes designed by Fred and George Miles.

Fred Miles flew his first aeroplane in 1929 and its successors broke numerous records in pre-war years. Best-known of the Miles types were the Magister basic trainer, on which thousands of wartime RAF pilots learned to fly, and the machine on which many progressed for advanced training, the Master.

Another wartime Miles product was the Messenger communications aircraft, used by General Montgomery among others.

Although the Miles name is almost entirely linked with light aircraft, in the 1940s the company designed great transatlantic airliners, tail-first types, and even partly built what was to have been the first supersonic aeroplane, the Miles M52. Sadly the government took fright at the risks and cancelled it in 1946.

In 1947 Miles ran into financial trouble and was bought by Handley Page. The brothers launched a new company which eventually became part of the Beagle light aircraft group.

Miles were innovators and in early post-war years turned to a very different field from aeroplanes – making Biro ballpoint pens.
Perhaps if they had persisted in that line it would have been more profitable than aircraft!

Mitsubishi A6M 'Zero'

most famous of Japanese fighters

The Zero, or Zero-Sen, was greatly feared by Allied pilots in the early months after Japan entered the war, but in fact it was not outstanding. Its light construction made it fast and manoeuvrable, but at a penalty of vulnerability when hit.

Its reputation for invincibility arose when it was pitted against poor Allied types such as the Brewster Buffalo. Once better American fighters like the Grumman Hellcat arrived, the Zero became outclassed.

Many Zeros ended their days as the mount of Kamikaze suicide pilots. Today Mitsubishi is again a leading military aircraft builder.

THE ONE-WAY MISSIONS

Japan resorted to Kamikaze ('Divine Wind') suicide attacks in the last 10 months of the war. Some 3,000 pilots sacrificed their lives, using obsolete fighters carrying a bomb or flying a specially designed rocket-propelled piloted bomb called the Ohka.

The results were poor for the loss of life involved – many ships were damaged and some sunk, but not one capital ship was destroyed.

The kamikaze pilots tend to be portrayed as fanatical volunteers (it is often hard to avoid 'volunteering' for wartime missions!), but they were still subject to human emotions.

One can only wonder about their thoughts and fears as they steeled themselves for that final mission.

NAMC YS-11

Japan's first post-war airliner

The 60-passenger YS-11 first flew in 1962, powered by two Rolls-Royce Dart turboprops.

182 were built, including an order from the American airline Piedmont, but the programme was not considered an unqualified success.

For the passengers, the windows were set a little too low; did the Japanese designers forget Western travellers are taller?

Nieuports

some of the finest Allied First World War fighters

Brothers Edouard and Charles de Niéport (they changed their name slightly in forming their company) were building racing aeroplanes as early as 1910. Both were killed in prewar accidents, but under designer Gustave Delage the firm built some of the best Allied wartime fighters.

Best known were the Nieuport 11 'Bébé' and the later Nieuport 17 biplanes. The former was a real lifesaver to the Allies, for it was almost alone in being able to match the dreaded Fokker monoplanes.

A machine-gun mounted above the top wing fired above the propeller and overcame the problem of interrupter gears. Many 'aces' in both France and Britain flew Nieuports.

Noorduyn Norseman
sturdily serving Canadian 'bush' pilots for 60 years

The Norseman was Robert Noorduyn's only design to go into production, but it has stood the test of time well: although it first flew in 1935 a number are still hard at work to this day, still engaged on the tough Canadian 'bush' flying for which they were designed.

The Norseman is a single-engine high wing aeroplane which can be fitted with wheels, floats or skis.

What happened to Glen Miller?

The wartime American bandleader disappeared over the English Channel in a Norseman.

Speculation has continued ever since about his fate, but the concensus is that he was unlucky enough to have been hit by a bomb jettisoned by a returning Allied bomber.

North American AT-6 Harvard
classic trainer for the world

Tens of thousands of wartime pilots flew at least some of their training on Harvards (or Texans in America). The Harvard was the first American aircraft bought in quantity by the RAF, with whom it served as an advanced trainer throughout the war and until 1955. More aggressively, it was also used to attack Mau-Mau terrorists in Kenya in the 1950s.

Over 20,000 Harvards were made, serving not only the USAAF, US Navy and the RAF, but also most Commonwealth countries. South Africa was still using Harvards up till 1995. Even Japan, which had taken out a prewar manufacturing licence, flew Harvards.

The Harvard was notorious for its howl – the propeller for the Pratt & Whitney Wasp engine reached supersonic speed at its tip. A number of these classic aircraft are now flown privately, and in America there are class races just for this type.

North American B-25 Mitchell
one of the best American wartime bombers

The twin-engine Mitchell, with characteristic twin tail-fins and tricycle undercarriage, was named after Billy Mitchell, a controversial prewar protagonist of air-power.

The B-25, which first flew in 1940, was widely used by the USAAF, the RAF, and by Russia. Its most famous raid was that mounted from an aircraft carrier against Japan in 1942. Some Mitchells were armed with a 75mm cannon, a huge weapon for airborne use. Intended to attack tanks or ships, it was not wholly successful; the gun had to be reloaded by hand after each shot!

Over 9,000 B-25s were made (some sources quote nearer 11,000). A number of countries flew the bomber until the late 1970s.

DOOLITTLE'S DANGEROUS MISSION

Famous pre-war racing pilot, Jimmy Doolittle, led the raid on Japan by 16 B-25s in April 1942. Take-off was from the carrier USS Hornet, a feat of airmanship in a type never designed for the purpose.

There was no hope of return – pilots had to force-land in China or Russia. There were casualties and bombing damage was limited, but there was enormous psychological effect – Japan was not invulnerable.

North American F-86 Sabre
classic early swept-wing fighter

The Sabre first flew in October 1947, and 6 months later became the first aircraft destined for production to exceed Mach 1 (in a shallow dive).

The F-86 proved crucial in Korea. Russian-built MiG-15s had outflown all Allied fighters, but arrival of the Sabre completely reversed the balance, to such effect that 8 MiGs were shot down for each F-86; much of the credit for this was due to better American pilot training and Second World War experience.

The Sabre was one of the most widely used of all jets, being used by many European countries including Britain (the RAF flew some 300), and among others Japan, Canada, and Australia. These last three countries built the type too. The standard engine was the General Electric J47, but Canada substituted the Avro Canada Orenda and Australia the Rolls-Royce Avon.

9,502 Sabres were built, including a carrier version for the US Navy which was called the Fury. The F-86 was one of the finest military aeroplanes of its era.

North American F-100 Super Sabre
worthy successor to the Sabre

A totally new design despite its name, the Super Sabre was the first fighter able to exceed Mach 1 on the level, a feat which was demonstrated on its very first flight, in 1953.

Twice the F-100 held the world speed record. On the first occasion the record was taken at 755 mph (1,215 kph) at the frightening height of 75 feet. Improved measuring equipment allowed all later records to be set at safer altitudes.

Early in its career the F-100 was grounded following several fatalities due to loss of control at speed. Major design changes were needed, but once completed the type served well for many years.

In Vietnam it was one of the major American combat aircraft – it has been claimed that more F-100 missions were flown in that conflict than the Mustang flew in World War Two.

North American P-51 Mustang
one of the finest wartime fighters

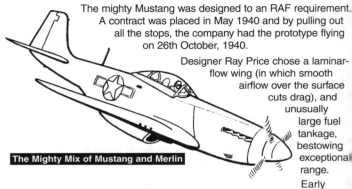

The mighty Mustang was designed to an RAF requirement. A contract was placed in May 1940 and by pulling out all the stops, the company had the prototype flying on 26th October, 1940.

Designer Ray Price chose a laminar-flow wing (in which smooth airflow over the surface cuts drag), and unusually large fuel tankage, bestowing exceptional range.

The Mighty Mix of Mustang and Merlin

Early Mustangs were powered by Allison liquid-cooled engines, but these lacked supercharging and were effective only at low level. The aeroplane became one of aviation history's classics when matched with the Packard-built Rolls-Royce Merlin, a combination considered by many to have been the best fighter of the war. Lest Spitfire fans take offence, it must be remembered the famous British fighter was designed over 4 years earlier.

The great range of the Mustang transformed daylight bombing operations over Germany, where losses were becoming grievous. It is said that when Luftwaffe leader Hermann Goering saw these single-seat fighters over Berlin he realised defeat was looming.

A curious development was the 1945 Twin Mustang, virtually two Mustangs joined together to give yet more range. Each fuselage held a cockpit, pilots being able to share the flying on long missions.

Mustangs were back in action against Communist ground positions in Korea. They often proved more suitable than jets when flying low amongst hills.

Astonishingly, this Second World War fighter was built again in small numbers in the late 1960s and early 1970s for export. 15,586 Mustangs were made. Many fly on in private hands, notably in America where it is popular for racing and delighting all who revel in the sight and Merlin sound of these classic fighters.

North American XB-70 Valkyrie
mighty Mach 3 bomber

This massive 6-engine machine was intended to replace the Boeing B-52. First flown in 1964, in many ways it was a most impressive technical achievement. However no production order was placed, largely due to the enormous cost of the complex machine. With hindsight it was probably just as well, for the B-70 would soon have become vulnerable.

Nowadays emphasis for survival is all on 'Stealth' technology, and it is interesting that the present-day Northrop B-2 bomber is subsonic.

Two prototypes were tested, but an accompanying F-104 pilot flew too close and hit the tail, so then there was one. The test programme ended in 1969.

Northrop Alpha
trendsetting fast metal airliner

Jack Northrop was one of the outstanding designers of the 1920s and '30s. His concept of building wings with multiple spars gave an enormous improvement to durability.

The Alpha was the first production aeroplane in the world to use 'stress-skin' metal construction (essentially the method used ever since). The 7-seat airliner cruised at 180 mph (290 kph) on a single Pratt & Whitney Wasp engine, matching most fighters of its day.

Alphas served well until the larger Douglas and Lockheed twins arrived to rule the airways.

Northrop B-2 Spirit
extraordinary 'stealth' bomber

Just a few years ago, bomber designers aimed for the highest possible speed to elude defences. Now all that has changed: the B-2 relies on making its 'radar signature' as small as possible by such means as careful shaping of surfaces, using absorbent paints, and shielding engine intakes and jet-pipes.

Speed is sacrificed, so the B-2 is subsonic – afterburning engines would give the game away. Compare this with the Mach 3 North American XB-70 above. Such technology has its price, and the B-2 is the most expensive aeroplane in history (so far!) at $1.3 billion each.

For comparison a First World War bomber cost around £2,000-£3,000. Not surprisingly, only 20 have been ordered.

Northrop F-5 and T-38
a quiet world-wide success story

The T-38 Talon was a supersonic trainer with two General Electric J85 turbojets, first flown in 1959. The F-5 Freedom Fighter and more advanced Tiger II were derived from the same basic design.

Never one of the most spectacular of military jets, equally they were less costly than the 'heavyweights' and consequently sold to the extent of several thousands throughout the world.

Northrop P-61 Black Widow
first purpose-designed night-fighter

Early in World War Two day fighters were sent aloft at night in a usually vain hunt for hostile bombers. Such methods as dropping flares (ineffective) and airborne searchlights (risky if the enemy fired back!) were tried, but most bombers escaped unscathed until airborne radar was developed.

The P-61 was designed to take the new compact radars (Britain had provided the technology). It was a twin-engine, twin tail-boom design, painted all black to suit its mission. Although not built in great numbers, Black Widows achieved reasonable success in both Europe and the Pacific.

Northrop YB-49
sensational tail-less jet bomber

Jack Northrop had been a devotee of dispensing with tails since the early 1930s – if good control can be achieved, drag will be lower. In 1946 he flew a large piston-powered bomber, the XB-35, but it suffered problems with its complex propeller drives. This at least was no problem with his real tour de force, his mighty YB-49 flying wing.

Powered by 8 Allison J35s buried neatly in the wing, it looked sensational when it flew in 1947, and would still appear impressive today. Alas, futuristic as it was, there were problems, a fatal accident to one prototype did not help, and it was not ordered into production.

The present-day B-2 bears a superficial resemblance to its predecessor of 40 years earlier, although the technology is worlds apart.

Panavia Tornado
European multinational strike aircraft

After many false starts at making an advanced European combat aeroplane, the Panavia consortium was formed in 1969 to build what later became the Tornado. Originally 5 countries took part, but eventually only Britain, Germany and Italy stayed the course.

British pilot Paul Millet made the first flight, in Germany, on 14th August, 1974. The crew looked embarrassed to be presented with flowers on landing, but such was continental custom.

Seven long years elapsed before Tornados reached the squadrons, but they were worth waiting for: it is one of the most impressive aeroplanes of its generation.

The Tornado was designed for very low-level operation and fitted with advanced terrain-following radar to allow the two crew to fly night or day in all weathers, needless to say placing total trust in their electronics. Britain also developed the F3 fighter version, something of a compromise in that it lacks the agility of the latest pure fighters, but effective nevertheless.

Engines are two RB199s, developed by Turbo-Union, another tri-national group linking Rolls-Royce with continental partners.

Tornados played a crucial role in the 1991 Gulf War, performing very low level missions to knock out Iraqi airfields, radars and similar strategic targets. Some 1,500 missions were flown by the RAF, but 6 aircraft and two crews were lost, a reflection of the hazardous nature of those operations.

Saudi Arabian Tornado fighter versions also took part with some success.

> *The Tornado brought together old enemies as friends.*
> *Former Messerschmitt and RAF pilots and designers*
> *worked side-by-side.*
> *Naturally there were disagreements but the result is a*
> *triumph of international organisation.*

Parnall Peto
daring submarine-based aviation

Parnall of Yate, near Bristol, built other firms' designs under licence but also produced some of their own, although few were made in quantity. The idea of designing an aeroplane to be launched from submarines generated little enthusiasm from the big firms – the market looked pretty limited! That left the field open to Parnall.

The tiny Peto seaplane was embarked on the submarine M2, emerging from its hangar when the vessel was on the surface, and launched when needed

Trials in 1926 were successful up to a point, being limited to calm seas. Some submariners questioned the wisdom of fitting a hangar with necessarily large door on a submarine, and tragically they were proved right when the M2 was lost with all hands in Lyme Bay.

Percival Gulls
choice of record-breakers and racers

Australian-born Edgar Percival broke from the British biplane tradition by designing a line of fast, good-looking monoplanes in the 1930s. The various Gulls were flown by many of the pre-war trailblazers like Jean Batten with her solo flights to South America, Australia, and New Zealand, and Alex Henshaw's record breaking flights to South Africa.

Over 500 of a wartime trainer and communications version, called the Proctor, were built. The Percival company itself was bought by shipping interests in 1944 and renamed Hunting Percival. A post-war piston-engine trainer, the Provost, was used by the RAF, but far more important was its jet derivative, described under Hunting Percival as the Jet Provost.

Edgar Percival himself had one more dabble at making aircraft with his EP9 of 1955 designed for agricultural work. 21 were sold.

Piasecki Helicopters
first widely-used twin-rotor helicopters

American Frank Piasecki was a pioneer of twin-rotor helicopters. They were widely used in Korea and Vietnam, and in civil use. Due to a characteristic cranked fuselage (to mount the rear rotor well above the forward one), they were known as the 'Flying Bananas'. A drive linked the rotors so that if either engine failed the other would turn both rotors.

After changes in company ownership, Piasecki became the Vertol division of Boeing, and their designs led to the hugely successful Chinook, for over 30 years one of the most important large helicopters in the world.

Pilatus Porter
the spritely Swiss performer

The Porter first flew in 1959 with a single piston engine. The 8-seater was designed with outstanding take-off and landing performance, as befitted the difficult terrain of its homeland. Two years later came the Turbo-Porter, as its name suggests using a turboprop engine. It was a world-wide success for both military and civil use.

American-built versions even served in Vietnam armed with cannon, rockets and all sorts of nasty accessories. The success of this aeroplane gave Pilatus the strength to buy the British Britten-Norman company in 1978 and add the enormously successful Islander to their range.

Piper Cub
classic American lightplane

Originally the Taylor Cub, the design and company were bought by William Piper in 1930. Of simple, high-wing, layout, early Cubs sold for just over $1,000 and became one of the most popular light aircraft of their era. In World War Two almost every American general flew between his units in Piper Cubs, and thousands were used for tactical observation and training.

Improved Cubs appeared after the war – owners were beginning to expect more than the stark unheated 75 mph (120kph) of the earlier versions. One modified Cub reached 30,203 feet (9,206 m) in 1951.

Eventually over 27,000 were made, laying the foundation for building Piper into one of the largest of light and business aeroplane manufacturers.

Porte (Felixtowe) flying-boats
splendid giants of the First World War

The fine flying-boats designed by naval engineer John Porte, and based partly on Curtiss machines, were among the largest aeroplanes of their day, although perversely he called one giant the 'Baby'!

They did sterling maritime patrol work for the Royal Naval Air Service. However the company did not long survive its founder's death in 1919 and loss of wartime contracts.

> *In 1917 a Porte flying-boat was used for a 'piggy-back'*
> *launch of a Bristol Scout in flight, making it a sort of aerial*
> *aircraft carrier, long preceding the much better known Mayo-*
> *Mercury experiments of 20 years later.*

Republic P-47 Thunderbolt
massive American wartime fighter

The 'Jug' was a formidable-looking fighter built around a large radial engine, a Pratt & Whitney R-2800. First flight was on 6th May 1941. The P-47 became one of the principal American fighters of the war years, widely used in both Europe and the Pacific. 15,683 were built, including some 830 for the RAF.

> The P-47 was a heavyweight by the standards of the day. It weighed about twice as much as an early Spitfire.
>
> As a result, rate of climb and low-level performance were poor, but it had an excellent turn of speed at altitude.
>
> Great care was therefore needed over tactics, but if handled skilfully it had a fine combat record. The heavy structure absorbed damage well and gave useful protection to the pilot.

Robinson helicopters
popular American light helicopters

Over 1,000 Robinson R22 and R44s have been built since 1975, making it one of the most popular machines for aerial work, business, and training.

However at the time of writing restrictions have been placed on the speeds and weather conditions for flying these helicopters following a series of accidents, although many owners are convinced problems have arisen by the way they have been flown rather than due to any fault in the designs.

Rockwell B-1B Lancer
American strategic jet bomber

The North American company was renamed Rockwell after a change of ownership. The B-1 was intended as a successor to the ageing Boeing B-52, and flew in 1974. The original highly complex B-1 was cancelled by President Carter in 1977, a controversial decision at the time but one which with hindsight was probably fortuitous: 'stealth' technology (see Northrop B-2) would soon have made it obsolete and vulnerable.

The aeroplane was resurrected as the simpler B-1B and put into production as a cruise missile carrier. 100 have been built. The engines are four General Electric F101 turbofans.

Royal Aircraft Factory SE5

one of the best British World War One aeroplanes

The government-owned Royal Aircraft Factory (later renamed Royal Aircraft Establishment to avoid confusion of initials when the Royal Air Force was formed in 1918) was a major supplier of early combat aeroplanes to the British services.

Some of their designs had poor reputations for combat handling and in some cases structural failure, but the SE5 was a winner. Designed by Henry Folland, later of Glosters and finally founder of his own company, the SE5 flew on 22nd November, 1916, powered by a 220 hp Hispano-Suiza H-5 engine.

After an inauspicious start – the second prototype broke up, killing the pilot – the structure was strengthened and the SE5 went on to become a wartime classic, with excellent performance and handling. The bulk of the 5,205 built were of the improved SE5a with more powerful Hispano-Suiza engine.

Some SE5s were used for ground attack with small bombs, anticipating the widespread such use of fighters in the next war.

> *A more peaceful use of SE5s came in the 1920s and '30s, when they were used for skywriting, whereby a skilled pilot could write a slogan or advertising message with his contrails ('vapour trails') in the sky.*
>
> *The technique was tricky, for the pilot could not see his own handiwork until it was complete. This rather harmless practice was later banned.*

Rutan homebuilts

revolutionary light aeroplanes

American designer 'Bert' Rutan totally ignored convention in conceiving his light aeroplanes. Traditional layouts and materials were discarded in favour of bizarre-looking but highly efficient tail-first designs (canards) made from foam and fibreglass. The materials were chosen largely for DIY construction at home.

His Vari-Ezi of 1975 reached 200 mph (322 kph) on just 100 hp. A spectacular flight was the first non-stop flight round the world without refuelling, in 1986. The specially-built 'Voyager' was flown by Bert's brother Dick Rutan and Jeana Yeager.

The 111ft (33.8 m) span aeroplane was demanding to fly and their 9-day flight was an epic of courage and endurance comparable to the great trailblazing flights of pre-war years.

Ryan NYP (New York-Paris)
Charles Lindbergh's mount

After Lindbergh tried various companies for an aeroplane without success, the little Ryan company finally offered to build one to his specification within 60 days. Designer Donald Hall produced a high-wing monoplane with a 220 hp Wright Whirlwind engine.

Lindbergh wanted the massive fuselage fuel tank in front of him, to reduce the danger in case of mishap, but this gave him virtually no forward view, other than obliquely through the side windows and via a periscope.

He took off from Roosevelt Field near New York in the 'Spirit of St. Louis' on 20th May, 1927. The flight took 33 hours, much of which in those pre-autopilot days was a battle to stay awake until his landing at le Bourget, Paris.

The aeroplane is preserved in the Smithsonian Museum, Washington, while a film replica is displayed at St. Louis airport.

> *Lindbergh settled on Ryan almost by chance: his original choice was a Bellanca but that company would 'sell' an aeroplane only on the absurd condition that they nominated the pilot!*
>
> *Lindbergh was naturally disenchanted.*

Saab fighters
world-class combat aircraft from Sweden

Saab was established in 1937, an earlier company of the same name having been formed in 1921 (cars started later, in 1949). Saab were the first in Europe to build a swept-wing fighter, the portly J-29 'Flying Barrel' of 1948. It was followed in the 1950s by the Saab 32 Lansen and the impressive 'double-delta' J-35 Draken of 1955, still in service 40 years later. In 1967 came the A-37 Viggen, a trendsetter in using a forward 'canard' control surface to aid handling, a feature now commonplace.

The current combat aircraft is the JAS-39 Gripen of 1988. Despite loss of the prototype in a crash, it continues the company's fine record of building first-class front-line aeroplanes. Every one of their post-war line has been a technical success, although export sales have been few.

An interesting feature is that all have been designed to operate from straight stretches of roads, allowing quick dispersal in times of threat.

Successful though these aircraft have been, Saab have wisely returned to commercial types in recent years (a post-war airliner, the 1946 Scandia, was made in small numbers).

The twin turboprop 340 of 1983, originally in association with Fairchild in America, and more recent and larger 50-58 seat Saab 2000 have sold well to airlines throughout the world.

Saunders-Roe (Saro) SR53 and 177
unique hybrid rocket/jet fighters

The ambitious SR53 with Armstrong Siddeley Viper jet for cruise and a de Havilland Spectre rocket for sprint flew in 1957. It was to have been followed by the SR177 operational fighter, which promised staggering performance for its day.

The SR53 performed well in tests, despite an unlucky fatal accident, but despite export orders at an advanced stage of negotiation the SR177 was cancelled in the short-sighted 1957 White Paper, which saw no further need for manned fighters. It was one of the great missed opportunities of British aviation.

Saunders-Roe Princess
mighty flying-boat

Following a long flying-boat tradition, Saro conceived the great 10-engine Princess to carry around 100 passengers on post-war Atlantic and Commonwealth routes. One Princess flew in 1952, but times had changed since the pre-war era of stately flying-boats. Now almost every city had an airport and the extra weight and drag of a flying-boat hull was too much to bear and compete with landplanes.

It was a pity, for the Princess was well engineered. The ten engines were Bristol Proteus turboprops, 8 in coupled pairs and two singles. The three Princesses built were stored until 1967. Many ideas for their use, even including one with an airborne nuclear reactor, came to nothing and eventually the inevitable sad decision was made to scrap them.

> *Soon after the first flight of the Princess, Geoffrey Tyson amazed the crowds at the Farnborough Air Show with steep low turns in this new and huge aeroplane.*
> *What they did not know was that far from being a demonstration of his confidence, he was wrestling with a problem on the powered controls (on which the Princess incidentally led the world) and was on the verge of losing control. Disaster was perilously close!*

Savoia-Marchetti SM55
pioneer of long-distance ocean travel

An unusual twin-hull flying-boat, the SM55 was used for two remarkable formation flights by Italian leader General Balbo.

In 1930 he took 14 to Brazil, with one loss, and in 1933 led 25 improved SM55X versions to Chicago and back. 23 returned safely, a fine feat of flying and organisation.

Savoia-Marchetti 79 Sparviero (hawk)
Italy's best wartime bomber

The 1934 trimotor SM79 was used for some pre-war record-breaking flights, and in less peaceful duties is considered to have been Italy's most effective wartime bomber. Some 1,330 were made.

The SM82 trimotor transport is likewise regarded as the best Axis transport. A few served with post-war airlines.

Scottish Aviation Pioneer and Twin Pioneer
sprightly take-off performers from Scotland

The Prestwick based company flew the Pioneer, sometimes called the Prestwick Pioneer, in 1950. It was a light transport with outstanding take-off ability – 225ft (68m) to take off and 200ft (60m) to land. A single 520 hp Alvis Leonides piston engine provided the power.

The larger Twin Pioneer followed in 1955, proving a more useful transport. Two of the same engines as the 'single' were used, although a few for export were fitted with Pratt & Whitney engines. 85 'Twin-Pins' were made; it is a pity the line was never developed further.

> *When the Pioneer was demonstrated at Farnborough, its short landing run was demonstrated in the original but effective way of landing across the runway and stopping within its width.*

Sepecat Jaguar
first collaborative front-line aircraft

The Anglo-French Jaguar was jointly built by BAC and Breguet (later Dassault), who formed the Sepecat company for the purpose. The two engines were likewise a joint Rolls-Royce and Turbomeca project, the Adour. First flown in 1968, the Jaguar entered French service in 1973, and with the RAF a year later.

Generally the collaboration has worked fairly well, although Dassault have sometimes been accused of 'pushing' sales of their own aircraft harder than the Jaguar!

After over 20 years service, the Jaguar remains in front-line ground attack service with its countries of origin, although its service life may be nearing an end. However in India it continues in production.

In the 1991 Gulf War, British and French Jaguars flew over 600 combat missions without a single loss.

Short Empire Flying-Boats
the graceful transports of a more leisurely age

When first flown in July 1936, the four-engine C class, or 'Empire' monoplane flying-boat was one of the most advanced aeroplanes in the world.

Imperial Airways were so confident in the design that they ordered 28 'off the drawing board' – before first flight, an unprecedented step at the time, although not unusual today.

The Empire boats and larger successors gave reliable service in peace and war, although with a fair number of accidents, until most airlines converted to landplanes by 1950.

**Short Empire Flying boat –
Air Travel at its Finest**

Last of all were two Sandringhams used by Australian airline Ansett to serve Lord Howe Island until the late 1960s, when the era of the great flying-boats ended for ever.

THE TRANSPORTS OF DELIGHT

Fitted out for 24 day passengers, or 16 sleeping, these lovely flying-boats offered a style of air travel never enjoyed before or since. The view from these high-wing machines cruising at relatively low altitude is unmatched by today's high-flying pressurised airliners.

Crew and passengers came to know each other, and even romances blossomed – not so easy in a thirteen-abreast jumbo! Many passengers mourned the passing of the Empire flying-boats.

Short Seaplanes
stalwarts of early naval flying

Eustace and Oswald Short started in aviation as early as 1901 – building balloons. Joined by older brother Horace they moved on to aeroplanes in 1909, building Wright biplanes under licence and becoming the first series producers of aircraft in the world.

Soon they started their own designs, including one of the first twin-engine aeroplanes in 1911. For much of its early history Shorts were associated with marine aviation, and their seaplanes were a mainstay of RNAS flying in the First World War. They were among the first to be flown from ships, to drop torpedoes, and to feature wing folding for storage on ships.

Over 1,000 Short seaplanes were made, mainly of the Type 184, which was widely used for reconnaissance and bombing.

SEAPLANES AND FLYING-BOATS

Many people think the terms 'seaplane' and 'flying-boat' to be synonymous, but they are in fact different: a seaplane rests on floats, with the fuselage supported clear of the water.

British seaplanes generally used twin floats but many American designs had a central large float with smaller ones below the wing for stability. In a flying-boat, the fuselage is a hull and rests in the water. It is more suitable for larger aircraft.

Nowadays water-based flying is confined to specialised uses such as 'bush' flying where there is plenty of water, and water-bombing of fires.

Short Silver Streak
pioneer of metal construction

This all-duralumin biplane was far ahead of its time when it appeared in 1920. Sadly the Air Ministry lacked the foresight of Eustace and Oswald Short, and only a few flights were authorised. Thus was a golden opportunity for Britain's aircraft industry thrown away.

Shorts' bold pioneering effort with the Silver Streak was frustrated to the extent that officialdom actually forbade them to demontrate it to export customers!

Short Skyvan, 330 and 360
ungainly but useful transports

Skyvan was conceived as a rugged light freighter. It first flew in 1963, but its potential was delayed by changing from piston engines to Turbomeca Astazou turboprops and finally Garrett AiResearch engines.

The Skyvan is totally utilitarian to look at, with slab-sided fuselage, high plank-like wing braced with struts, fixed undercarriage, and rectangular twin fins. Nevertheless, Skyvans proved highly practical and served well in difficult terrain all over the world, including with American forces in Vietnam.

The Shorts 330 (for some reason the company made a habit of putting a final 'S' on their name for a time) was a larger 30-seat airliner, retaining the angular looks but plushier inside. The later 360 took 30 passengers and made some concession to its appearance with a more streamlined single fin. They sold in reasonable numbers.

One industry observer on seeing the first Skyvan commented "That's the most aerodynamic shed I've ever seen!"

Short Stirling
first of the wartime heavy bombers

The Stirling might have been a great aeroplane had its design not been restricted by two Air Ministry compromises. The first stipulated that it double as a transport, which limited the size of bomb-bay and prevented Stirlings from carrying any bomb larger than 2,000lb (Lancasters could carry one of 22,000lb.) The second limitation was that the wingspan be not more than 100 feet (30m) to fit within standard hangars of the day.

How bitterly Stirling crews must have regretted this! Not only did the limited altitude they could reach expose them to more danger from gunfire below, but they also had to contend with bombs falling from other bombers above. On the credit side, handling and manoeuvrability were good.

Before flying the Stirling, Shorts took the unusual step of flying a half-scale version to check handling. Everything was exactly scaled – except the pilot! First flight of the Stirling itself was in May 1939, but was marred by a brake failure on landing which wrote off the prototype.

Stirlings started operations in February 1941 and continued as bombers until 1944. 2,381 were built, all powered by Bristol Hercules engines. Later in its career, the Stirling was used for glider-towing, parachute dropping, and as a transport (so that misguided compromise had some use after all). A few even served as primitive post-war airliners, but not for long and not a single one was preserved.

The Stirling was easily distinguished from the other British 'heavies' by its single fin, and on the ground by a long, stalky undercarriage; this feature arose from a late demand for a higher wing angle of attack on landing, leaving as a legacy a rather weak undercarriage.

> *Alan Wheeler, Commandant of the trials unit at Boscombe Down, tested a Stirling at maximum weight. The load was a complement of paratroopers.*
>
> *Someone had miscalculated the weights, for Wheeler had a desperate battle to lift off and climb away. Even after he had gained some height he was in trouble and was about to order the paratroopers to jump when he sensed the aircraft responding.*
>
> *It was as well he withheld the order as it turned out the soldiers had left their parachutes behind!*

Short Sunderland
illustrious wartime flying-boat

Developed from the Empire flying-boats, the Sunderland proved invaluable in escorting convoys and for anti-submarine work. Heavily armed with up to 18 guns, it was nicknamed 'The Flying Porcupine' by German aircrews who treated it with respect.

However, as with all flying-boats, it was vulnerable to attack from below, so in time of danger crews would fly close to the surface of the sea. Sunderlands accounted for a number of U-boats, but even more important was preventing submarine attacks by their presence. The one major limitation of the Sunderland was that it lacked the range of Liberators or Catalinas for ocean patrol.

Early in the war some notable rescues of men in the sea were made, but because of the risk the practice was later forbidden. Some crews disobeyed orders rather than leave men to perish in the sea, risking their lives if they failed and the wrath of their superiors if they succeeded.

Sunderlands gave valuable service long after the end of the war: in 1948 they served on the Berlin Airlift, landing on a lake in the city until winter ice formed. The RAF retired their last Sunderlands in 1959. Last to go were those of the Royal New Zealand Air Force which flew on until 1967.

Short Tucano

today's standard RAF basic trainer

For some years the RAF practised 'all-jet' training. Later it was found more economical to handle initial training on small propeller driven types such as Bulldogs, but it might still have looked a backward step when the long-serving Jet Provosts were replaced by turboprop trainers.

However the Tucano was chosen because it handled like a jet but at far lower cost. The Tucano is adapted from a design by the Brazilian Embraer company, modified by Shorts to suit RAF requirements, needless to say at much cost and with long delay. Deliveries started in 1987. The engine is a Garrett TPE331 of 1,100 hp.

The last Tucano was completed in 1993, and sadly the end of the line also marked the end of 84 years of aeroplane building by Shorts. The firm, part of the Bombardier group since 1989, now concentrates on subcontract work and missiles.

Sikorski airliners

the first with four engines

Russian pioneer Igor Sikorski flew his 'le Grand' biplane in 1913. It was the world's first 4-engine aeroplane. He followed it with the even more ambitious Ilya Mourometz in 1914. An unusual feature was an outside promenade deck above the rear fuselage. One wonders how many passengers were brave enough to stroll along it, or hardy enough in a Russian winter. Some 75 were built, but employed as bombers, giving good service.

Sikorski emigrated to America and produced a line of fine flying-boats, before turning to the speciality for which he became most famous, the helicopter.

Sikorski helicopters
world leaders in rotary-winged flight

Igor Sikorski built a helicopter as early as 1909, but the idea was ahead of available technology. He returned to rotary wings in the late 1930s, and his VS-300 established the now classic layout of a main rotor and smaller tail rotor to stop the whole machine spinning round from the engine torque.

The VS-300 first flew under tether on 14th September 1939, but becoming airborne in a helicopter is the easy bit: the harder task is controlling it, and much painstaking development lay ahead.

The R-4 of 1942 is considered the first production helicopter, but it was the S-51 (called Dragonfly in Britain where it was the first of many Sikorskis built by Westland) which really established the company as a large-scale producer of these machines.

Its successors include the S-61 Sea King, used widely for military and airline use, but best known as a backbone of rescue services all over the world.

THE MERCIFUL HELICOPTER

Whenever there have been disasters in recent years, succour has come from the skies thanks to the versatile helicopter.

Many hundreds of thousands have been saved from floods, earthquakes, shipwreck, mountains, or almost every conceivable mishap.

Moreover disasters tend to happen in the vilest of weather, often stretching the skill and bravery of crews to almost unbelievable limits.

Sopwith Camel
classic fighter of World War One

After building the well regarded Pup 'Scout' (predecessor of the true fighter), Sopwith produced the agile Camel which appeared in 1917. The Clerget rotary engine was mounted in a very short nose, putting the weight near the centre of gravity and conferring outstanding manoeuvrability. The guns were mounted in a 'hump' in front of the cockpit, hence its name.

The Camel proved one of the most effective combat aeroplanes of its day, despite tricky handling due to the rotating mass of the engine. 5,490 Camels were built, and accounted for 1,294 enemy aircraft. That flown by 'Billy' Barker, VC, number B6313, was responsible for 48 'kills', believed to be the highest number for any individual aircraft in the history of air warfare.

Some Camels flew from ships or from towed lighters, mainly against Zeppelins, with some success, although they had to land at an aerodrome. There were even trial launches from an airship.

The Sopwith company, reliant entirely on military work, closed soon after the war but reformed as Hawker.

SPAD SVII and XIII
among the best of World War One fighters

These French fighters entered service in 1916 and earned a formidable name for their strength and manoeuvrability. Some 10,000 SPADS were made in Britain, France and Russia. The engine was a Hispano-Suiza 8A.

Stinsons
leading pre-war American civil aeroplanes

Stinsons, formed in 1926, were a real family business; two brothers and two sisters were all pilots! Stinsons were popular private-owner and record-breaking aircraft.

The first non-stop aeroplane transatlantic flight to land in Britain was by a Stinson Detroiter in 1927. The company later merged with Consolidated.

> *The crew of the transatlantic Detroiter, William Brock and Edward Schlee, relied for their navigation over Britain on a page from a school atlas.*

Sud-Est Alouette
pioneering turbine helicopter

The French Sud-Est company were one of the first to see the advantages of linking turbine power to helicopters, no doubt partly thanks to the nearby Turbomeca company with their lightweight small turbines, including the Artouste used in the Alouette. The first piston-powered Alouette flew in 1951, the turbine version following four year later.

The pioneering effort was well rewarded, for over 2,000 were built in France, Switzerland, Romania and India.

Sud-Est (later Sud and Aerospatiale) Caravelle
first short-haul jet airliner

When the Caravelle flew on 27th May 1955 it set a new design trend in mounting the two Rolls-Royce Avon engines on the rear fuselage. The advantages were an efficient wing uncluttered by pods, and a quiet cabin. The layout was widely copied for a time, but later designers reverted to wing-mounted engine pods as there was a weight penalty with rear engines. To save time, the nose section of the Comet was used.

The Caravelle became a most popular airliner, not least with passengers thanks to its quietness, though this benefit did not extend to those on the ground! 280 were sold, including 20 to United Airlines in America, who used them on a first-class only service for some years.

Later versions replaced the Avons with Pratt & Whitney JT8Ds turbofans. The structure proved strong enough on one occasion to survive collision with a light aircraft, the engine of which together with the dead pilot remained lodged in the Caravelle's cabin until landing. The success of the Caravelle did much to help establish the Airbus series of airliners.

> *A Caravelle passenger, glancing back into the engine intake behind him, was alarmed to see a large screwdriver lodged across the vanes in front of the engine. He alerted the crew, who thought there was less chance of it becoming dislodged if the engine was left running.*
> *It remained in place until landing, when the jolt knocked it into the engine.*

Sukhoi fighters
potent Russian combat aircraft

Less well known than the famous MiG family, Sukhoi designs have nevertheless formed much of Russian front-line strength since the early 1950s. Sukhoi piston aeroplanes were not outstanding, and the design team was actually closed in 1949.

When revived in 1953, it produced the swept-wing Su-7 'Fitter' (like most Soviet aircraft of the time, NATO code-names were used when true identities were unknown), which became a principal Eastern Bloc fighter. Ever since, Sukhoi fighters and ground attack fighters have formed a major part of the Russian armoury. As a generalisation, Russian combat aircraft have matched their Western counterparts in performance but lagged behind in engine design and electronics.

Sukhoi Su26 and 31
astounding aerobatic mounts

As a total departure from their thundering jets, Sukhoi introduced their little Su-26 to aerobatic competition in 1984. Their agility is almost unbelievable, with structures stressed to take up to 26g and capable of rolling at 400ft. a second (it needs an exceptional pilot to demonstrate its potential too!).

Supermarine Spitfire
the aeroplane which needs no introduction!

Perhaps the most famous military aeroplane of all time, the Spitfire, with its partner-in-arms the Hurricane, played a crucial role in defending Britain from invasion in 1940, and indeed in preserving the world at large from tyranny.

Designer Reginald Mitchell started work on his advanced fighter in the early 1930s. Whilst convalescing in Germany from treatment for cancer, he met various aviation personalities and became convinced they were preparing for war. He redoubled his efforts, realising that his creation would have a vital role in the expected conflict.

First flight was on 6th March 1936 at the hands of test pilot 'Mutt' Summers (there is some doubt over the exact date due to loss of records in a bombing raid – some historians quote the previous day). The Spitfire was powered by a single Rolls-Royce Merlin, originally of around 1,000 hp, although this power was to double over the war years.

8 machine-guns were fitted, and it was to house these that Mitchell designed the graceful elliptical wing which was to make the Spitfire so easily recognisable to expert and lay people alike – in fact post-war tests showed it to be a remarkably efficient wing at high speed.

Mitchell saw his great design fly, but never lived to see its immortal place in history, for the cancer returned and he died in 1937. By then the aeroplane had been named 'Spitfire'; the name caught the public imagination, but sadly its originator is unknown. Mitchell himself disliked the name, possibly because it had been used before for a rather undistinguished Supermarine fighter.

Production at first was painfully slow – that wing shape was complex to make – and there was even talk of cancelling Spitfire orders and substituting Hurricanes. However the production lines finally started churning them out, but only just in time.

In the Battle of Britain there were fewer Spitfires than Hurricanes, but they were blessed with the vital extra speed which enabled them to tackle German fighters on even terms. As far as possible, Hurricanes would attack the bombers while the faster Spitfires took care of the fighters, but it rarely worked out as simple as that! Most historians now consider the Spitfire to have been superior to its principal opponent at the time, the Messerschmitt Bf109.

The Spitfire

Immortal Symbol of Britain's Defiance

The Spitfire was continually developed until production ended after 22,759 had been built. Higher powered Merlins, and later Griffons, wing and aileron improvements, and cannon armament, all kept the Spitfire a match for its opponents, apart from a short period when the German Focke-Wulf 190 had the edge.

Speed increased by over 100 mph (160 kph) over the war years. It was one of the few types in full production at both the beginning and end of the war – a tribute to the dedicated work of Supermarine and Rolls-Royce engineers.

A naval version, the Seafire, was developed for carrier use. It was flown on many highly successful operations, but its narrow undercarriage and tricky view on the approach made it less than ideal for use at sea.

The part played by the Spitfire in history is so well known it hardly needs recounting. However it should always be remembered that it was not the Spitfire which won battles: it was the men who flew it, built it, and kept it flying. Behind every sortie there was gnawing fear, and all too often terrible injuries or death. Even so, many who flew it on operations recall it with affection: as one leading wartime pilot put it "I started the war on Spitfires, I ended it flying the same aircraft – I would not have had it any other way."

Supermarine Walrus
rescue saviour at sea

Although overshadowed by the same company's famous Spitfire, the little Walrus or 'Shagbat' played its own vital wartime role by plucking several thousand airmen and sailors from the sea.

Largely under Reginald Mitchell's design, Supermarine had made a fine range of pre-war flying-boats: the large Southampton biplanes gave 10 years of exemplary service to the RAF from 1925, and the later Stranraer served well into World War Two, with a handful flying on in civil use in Canada into the 1960s.

The Walrus was a small biplane amphibian with a single Bristol Pegasus engine driving a pusher propeller. A later version with tractor (front) propeller was called the Sea Otter. Initially its main use was in being catapulted from ships to 'spot' for the fleet. However it is best known for its part in the air-sea rescue service.

Many courageous rescues were made including one in the middle of a minefield. Sometimes there were so many men to pick up that the Walrus was unable to take off, in which case the pilot had to taxi home – in one instance for 50 miles over 5 hours! Walrus crews would save friend or foe alike. Like other amphibians, there are persistent tales, some probably apocryphal, others believed to be true, of pilots alighting on water with the wheels down, or conversely on land with them raised.

THE UNSUNG HEROES

Battle of Britain pilots may have received their rightful public acclaim, but Walrus crews were typical of the many doing unglamorous but dangerous and vital work throughout the war.

Tupolev ANT-20 'Maxim Gorki'
Russian pre-war giant

Andrei Tupolev was a pioneer of metal construction, and exploited its strength to build a series of outsize aeroplanes in the 1920s and '30s, culminating in the ANT-20.

This aircraft had a 260ft. (79m) wingspan and needed eight engines to haul itself airborne. The engineering marvel of its time was dedicated to no more worthy purpose than spreading propaganda with loudspeakers, for this was in Stalinist Russia.

Named after the writer Maxim Gorki, the great machine came to an untimely end when a fighter pilot, indulging in unauthorised aerobatics, collided with it, killing all on board.

More modest versions with six engines went into production as transports and served until 1945.

Tu-95 'Bear'
Russia's cold war 'eyes' on the West

The 'Bear' was unusual in being one of very few propeller driven aeroplanes to feature sharply swept wings. Developed as a bomber, the 'Bear' became familiar to Western interceptor pilots on its regular probes to test defences, flying just up to national airspaces to assess how fast fighters would respond.

An airliner version, the Tu-114, entered service for a short time. The 12,000 hp Kuznetsov turboprops drove propellers which reached supersonic speed at the tips.

> A photograph taken by a fighter which had intercepted a 'Bear' clearly shows a crewman holding up a bottle from which he was drinking; his choice of beverage? – decadent Western Pepsi-Cola!

Tu-104
the world's second jet airliner in service

When Russian leaders Bulganin and Khruschev visited London in 1956, they sprang a surprise by arriving in a jet airliner hitherto unknown in the West.

Developed from a swept-wing jet bomber, the Tu-16 'Badger', the Tu-104 was the second jet airliner in the world to enter regular passenger service. Powered by two Mikulin turbojets, the Tu-104 carried around 100 passengers. About 200 were made and handled much of Aeroflot's international traffic. For 3 years it was the only jet airliner in service anywhere.

A smaller-scale 56-seat version was also built, the Tu-124, which started services in 1962. The Tupolev company has been one of the principal Russian airliner builders over the last 40 years.

Tu-144
Russia's supersonic airliner

The Tu-144 first flew on 31st December 1968, making it the first supersonic airliner to fly. Powered by 4 Kuznetsov turbofans, the aircraft looked superficially like Concorde, and was often dubbed 'Concordski'.

A highly publicised fatal crash at the 1973 Paris Air Show demonstrated that all was not going smoothly with the programme, and services did not start till December 1976; even then they were largely confined to mail and freight carrying.

Before long the Tu-144 was quietly withdrawn from service and has never flown since, although at the time of writing there is a possibilty of using one for some research work in America.

Vickers FB5 Gunbus
beginning of the armed aeroplane

The Gunbus was a two-seat biplane with the gunner placed in the nose, ahead of the pilot. To give him a clear field of fire, the engine was mounted behind the crew and drove a pusher propeller. The Gunbus was developed from a 1913 design, the EFB1 (Experimental Fighting Biplane), named Destroyer.

Although it crashed on its first flight, it was notable in two respects: it was of all-metal construction, and was the first aeroplane to carry a gun, a Vickers (naturally!) in the nose. The Gunbus was widely used early in the war, but once the Fokker fighters appeared the slow two-seater was no match for them and the Gunbus was withdrawn in 1915.

Vickers Valiant
first of the 'V-Bombers'

At a time of 'cold war' tension, development of 4-engine jet bombers was given priority – so much so that no less than four such types were flown of which three went into service, the 'V-Bombers'. It seems almost unbelievable extravagance now.

The Valiant was first flown by Mutt Summers in May 1951. The prototype was lost in an accident the following January, in which the co-pilot was killed.

In October 1956 a Valiant dropped Britain's first atomic bomb, and later would do the same with the country's hydrogen bomb. At around the same time, the type was used 'in anger' during the Suez operations. 104 Valiants were built. The engines were Rolls-Royce Avons.

In 1964 the fleet was switched to low-level operations, when it became clear that bombers would no longer survive in Soviet airspace at high level. The stress on the structure caused by continuous low flying led to wing spar fatigue and the Valiants were withdrawn in 1965.

Vickers VC10
the fine airliner killed by the national airline

Vickers tried twice to enter the long-range jet airliner market: the first time was with the Vickers 1000 with four Rolls-Royce Conway turbofans (then called 'by-pass engines') buried in the wings. The prototype was partly built in 1955 when it was cancelled by the government.

The company tried again with the VC10, which also used Conways but this time mounted on the rear fuselage. The programme was launched on the basis of substantial orders from the long-haul airline BOAC (later merged into British Airways). The orders included both standard and lengthened Super VC10s, although the latter were twice shortened, becoming progressively less 'Super'!, before the airline decided what they wanted.

One of BOAC's requirements was for better take-off performance than a Boeing 707 for certain Commonwealth routes with small airports; by the time it was ready for service, the airports had been enlarged and the poor VC10 was burdened with extra weight and cost to meet a need which no longer existed.

First flight was in 1962, test pilot Jock Bryce commenting that "It was the best flight I have ever had in a VC10". Alas, by then BOAC had a new chairman who publicly denigrated the economics of the VC10, ignoring its passenger appeal from its rear-mounted engines and hence quiet cabin.

When it entered service it did indeed fly much fuller than the rival Boeing 707s and Douglas DC-8s and it proved a well-engineered airliner, but the damage had been done: just 54 were sold. The survivors are now flown as tankers by the RAF.

Vickers Viking
early post-war airliner

Vickers were one of many companies which saw a huge market in replacing the thousands of war-surplus Douglas DC-3s (Dakotas) plying the world's air routes. Their offering was the portly-looking Viking, conceived as a derivative of the Wellington bomber with the same two Bristol Hercules engines, although in the end there was little Wellington left in the airliner.

First flown in 1945, it was fairly successful with 163 sales, to which may be added 263 of the similar RAF Valetta transports (for some reason the spelling differs from the Maltese city) and 163 Varsity trainers.

However the aeroplane it was supposed to replace long outlived it: the last Vikings had gone by the mid-1960s, but 30 years later many DC-3s are still flying!

> In 1950 a bomb aboard a Viking blew a large hole in the fuselage, and worse still, severed the elevator control.
>
> The pilot, Captain Harvey, found he could maintain some pitch control by varying engine power, and by a remarkable feat of airmanship achieved a safe landing.

"GONE RATHER QUIET"

A VC-10 flight engineer committed the worst sin of his profession by mishandling the fuel system and shutting down all four engines in flight. The crew used an emergency turbine spun by the windflow to provide electrical power and restart the engines. It is as well they did restart promptly, for the turbine itself then failed!

The words of the captain are not recorded, perhaps fortunately, but those of another captain in similar circumstances were. He turned to his hapless engineer and remarked "gone rather quiet, hasn't it?"

Vickers Vimy
pioneer of the long-distance air routes

The Vimy has an unrivalled place in air exploration, for the type was used in the first non-stop Atlantic crossing, the first flight from Britain to Australia, and most of the first flight to South Africa.

The Vimy was designed by Rex Pierson, who was responsible for Vickers aircraft until the 1945 Viking, as a twin-engine bomber with Rolls-Royce Eagle engines. The prototype flew in 1917, just 4 months after the start of design. It just missed war operations, but it gave long service with the RAF. Including Virginias and Victorias, which were virtually developments of the same design, some flew on as late as 1944 and were even used for night bombing in North Africa in the Second World War.

Conqueror of Oceans and Continents

The Vickers Vimy

Distinguished as its service record was, the real place of the Vimy in history lies with its great trailblazing flights. The first and most famous was the Atlantic crossing by John Alcock and Arthur Whitten-Brown from Newfoundland to Ireland on 14-15th June, 1919. The 16 hour flight took the two aviators through dreadful weather and control was lost on at least one occasion, being regained only just above the sea.

Brown repeatedly had to reach out to clear ice from the instruments (more extravagant accounts have him walking along the wings to clear it from the radiators). The spot chosen for landing at Clifden in Ireland after all their hardships looked firm but proved to be a bog, resulting in the Vimy tipping on its nose. The repaired Vimy is now displayed in the Science Museum, London.

In December of the same year Ross and Keith Smith with two crew set off for Australia, which they reached 28 days later in an epic of skill and improvisation.

In February 1920 Pierre van Ryneveld and Quintin Brand left on the third great Vimy flight, this time to South Africa. They crashed in the Sudan, and borrowed another Vimy from the RAF, who may have rued their generosity for this one was damaged in Southern Rhodesia. However those pioneers were determined men, for they borrowed yet another aeroplane, a DH9, to complete their flight to Cape Town. All 6 pilots on these flights were knighted,but in a tragic coincidence both Jack Alcock and Ross Smith were killed soon afterwards in separate accidents, both involving Vickers Viking amphibians (not the Viking described above).

Air Ministry and company policy liked alliterative aircraft names e.g. Vickers types usually began with V. By the 1930s they were struggling to find enough such names and considered such improbable ones as Villain, Vandal, and even Virago ('abusive woman!')

Vickers Viscount
best-selling British airliner

George Edwards (later Sir George), the successor to Rex Pierson as head of design at Vickers, took the bold step of building the Viscount around turbine power. The prototype was a 32-seater, powered by four Rolls-Royce Dart turboprops. First flight was on 16th July 1948 in the experienced hands of Mutt Summers, who 12 years earlier had taken the Spitfire into the air for the first time. On 29th July 1950 this aeroplane was put into scheduled service between London and Paris, and later Edinburgh, by BEA.

These were the first turbine powered passenger services in the world. Full services with the larger 53-seat 700 Series Viscount started in April 1953. The aircraft was highly popular for its freedom from vibration (standing pencils on end was a favourite party piece), large windows, and its speed; claims that its cabin was quiet were more debatable.

Vickers Viscount

Brought Turbine Power to the Airlines

Orders flowed in from all over the world, including landmark sales to Trans Canada (now Air Canada) and the American airline Capital (later merged with United). These were the first significant airliner sales in North America by any European company.

Larger 800 Series Viscounts followed and sales eventually reached 444, the last 6 being the first Western aeroplanes delivered to Communist China. A handful remain in airline service. However many in the industry believed the Viscount could have been developed further and been even more successful; perhaps it was not done for fear of harming its larger successor, the Vanguard, of which only 43 were sold.

The Viscount was a daring and deservedly successful venture. The structure was perhaps let down by its single spar wing, already dated in the 1940s and the cause of expensive re-sparring in later life. Even so, one major airline described the Viscount as "By far the best aircraft we ever operated".

POWER BEHIND THE VISCOUNT

The story of the Viscount is closely bound up with that of its engine, the Rolls-Royce Dart. It was an act of faith when Vickers chose the engine, for at the time it was 30% overweight and 40% under power!

It is even said that on its first run it refused to start until a fitter pushed a welding torch through an igniter plug hole. Whether or not this is true, Rolls-Royce engineers pulled out the stops and turned the Dart into one of the most reliable engines of its time. Over 7,000 were made for a variety of aircraft types.

A Viscount on a coastal route landed at a diversion airport due, the passengers were told, to bad weather at their destination.

It soon transpired the weather had been perfect, and the story unravelled: due to some aberration the crew had set a course straight out to sea, and when the error was realised they had only enough fuel to reach the nearest coastal airfield.

Vickers Wellington
sturdy wartime bomber

The Wellington was probably the best British bomber in the early part of World War Two, and it gave excellent service even after the four-engine 'heavies' had largely supplanted it.

The Wellington was designed by Barnes Wallis of Dambusters bouncing bomb fame. The structure was of an unusual lattice type which he called 'Geodetic'. It had already been used on his single-engine bomber, the Wellesley, which had performed some notable long-distance flights. This structure proved robust in withstanding severe damage – in one instance a Wellington lost 6 feet of wing after hitting an obstacle at low level; the pilot was unaware of the damage until after landing! Another reached home after losing 10 feet of wing in a collision.

However the Geodetic structure did not take kindly to glider towing: after towing a Horsa the Wellington was reputed to have stretched $1\frac{1}{2}$ feet!

First flight was on 15th June 1936. The engines were two Bristol Pegasus; later Rolls-Royce Merlins, Pratt and Whitney Twin Wasps, or Bristol Hercules would provide more performance.

Early in the war the Air Staffs believed Wellingtons and other bombers carried enough guns to look after themselves in daylight. They were tragically wrong and on some missions half the Wellingtons were shot down.

Not even the bravest can take those odds for long, but it took some time for the Air Staffs to accept that unescorted bombers could not survive in daytime. The Germans made the same miscalculation at first). Operations were switched to night flying, but accuracy was poor at first.

One Wellington suffered a wing fire after being hit, whereupon crew member Jimmy Ward climbed out on to the wing to stuff it out, earning a well-deserved VC.

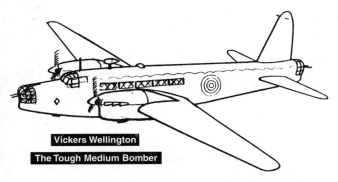

Vickers Wellington
The Tough Medium Bomber

Wellingtons proved versatile; some were used for torpedo-bombing, called 'Fishingtons', while others carried a 48 foot (15m) electromagnetic coil to detonate magnetic mines. The safe height was calculated theoretically but the first trials were a test of faith!

The Warwick was essentially an enlarged Wellington, little used in its intended role as a bomber but employed usefully as a lifeboat carrier for air/sea rescue. A four-engine derivative, the Windsor, did not enter service but it did incorporate the advanced feature of rearward-facing guns in 'barbettes' behind the engine nacelles, remotely controlled.

Another development which did not enter service but paved the way for the future was the 'High-altitude Wellington' which featured a pressure cabin, giving an appearance like an elephant seal, and highly supercharged engines. Changed needs led to its abandonment, which was perhaps as well as it would have been difficult to bale out from the pressure cabin.

11,460 Wellingtons were built, the highest total for any British bomber. The aeroplane was well liked by crews, largely thanks to its reputation for bringing them back after damage which would have been fatal to other types.

"GIVE US THE TOOLS TO DO THE JOB"

The Wellington structure was well designed for fast production: a propaganda film showed a Wellington being built from scratch to first flight in 24 hours.

> *The Wellington was universally known as the Wimpy. The name came from a character in a Popeye cartoon, J. Wellington Wimpy.*

Voisins
pioneers from France

Brothers Gabriel and Charles built gliders soon after learning of the Wright Brothers' trials. In 1907 they moved on to box-kite style powered biplanes, and they were amongst the first to offer aeroplanes for sale.

Early Voisins had no lateral control; not until 1910 were ailerons fitted. Despite this handicap, and the brothers seeming ability to fall out with their customers, Voisins were widely used by pioneer aviators.

During the First World War several thousand sound but conservatively designed Voisins, nicknamed the 'Chicken Coops', formed a major element of the French air services.

Vought F4U Corsair
probably the best naval fighter of World War Two

The distinctive Corsair with its cranked 'inverted gull' wing, to allow clearance for a large propeller, first flew in May 1940. The engine was a 2,000 hp Pratt & Whitney R-2800.

Its flying history started poorly with a crash on the 5th flight, and at first it was deemed unsuitable for carrier use by the US Navy, but it was to redeem itself with a fine combat record.

12,571 'Bent-wing Birds' were built, of which 2,012 were supplied to the Royal Navy. 2,140 Japanese aircraft were claimed by F-4U pilots against 189 losses of their own, a most favourable ratio of 11:1. Corsairs were still in combat in Korea, one accounting for a MiG-15 jet.

Production continued till 1952 and the aeroplane remained in US Navy service until the 1960s, and in France till 1965.

Vought F-8 Crusader
excellent carrier jet fighter

The 1955 Crusader was a mainstay of US Navy operations for two decades, and played a major role in Vietnam.

An unusual feature, and a 'first' on a production aircraft, was a variable-incidence wing, whereby the angle the wing was set on the fuselage could be adjusted. One setting was suitable for high speeds, while the other allowed a better view during the demanding approach to the carrier.

Two incidents involving Crusaders almost defy belief, but are well documented.

In the first, in 1960, a pilot had reached 5,000 feet when he realised he had launched with the wings folded! After discussion with superiors on deck, he did not attempt to open the wings but elected to land with them folded. It says much for the aeroplane's handling that such a feat was possible.

In 1963 Stuart Harrison experienced an engine failure shortly before landing on the carrier. Instead of ejecting he performed the near-impossible by landing on the deck 'dead-stick', probably the only time this has ever been done on a carrier.

Westland helicopters
Britain's principal line of rotary-wing aircraft

Westland took out a licence to build Sikorski helicopters in 1947, and soon afterwards concentrated entirely on this form of flight. The first such to be licence-built was the S-51, which Westland christened 'Dragonfly', followed by the S-55 (Whirlwind), S-58 (Wessex) and the S-61 Sea King, widely used for anti-submarine work, carrying troops, and in the role best-known to the public, sea and mountain rescue.

However when they promoted the Blackhawk attack helicopter, a political crisis occurred, popularly known as the 'Westland Affair', in which ministers favouring a wholly European programme resigned.

Westland have also produced original designs, notably the Lynx twin turbine helicopter, which since 1977 has been flown by the British services from both land and ships; in the latter role it was successfully used in the Falklands to attack or capture Argentine ships. The engines are two Rolls-Royce Gems.

Westland further expanded by taking over the helicopter interests of Bristol, Fairey, and Saunders-Roe. For a long time the company was virtually the only British company in the field, until British Aerospace took an interest in military helicopters.

A Whirlwind helicopter suffered a rotor shaft failure in 1967 and crashed.

The loss of the four crew was tragic enough, but it was a matter of pure chance that the occupants did not include the helicopter's owner – the Queen

Westland Lysander

legendary foundation for wartime clandestine operations

Designer 'Teddy' Petter produced a most distinctive-looking machine to meet a requirement for army co-operation work. The high lozenge-shaped wing had large slots and flaps to give remarkable take-off and landing performance.

From the fixed undercarriage sprouted stub wings, on which could be mounted machine-guns or small bombs. The Lysander was first flown by Harald Penrose in June 1936. The engine was a Bristol Mercury radial. The aeroplane proved versatile and was used for artillery spotting, ground attack, and for air-sea rescue (in which role Lysanders were known as the 'Salvation Navy').

Inevitably crews of these slow machines suffered heavy losses, although one Lysander observer managed to shoot down a Heinkel 111.

Lysanders Landed Agents at Night in Enemy Territory

By far the most famous use of these unusual aircraft was in landing and collecting agents from enemy territory. Operating at night into tiny fields marked out by friendly (it was hoped!) resistance fighters using torches or flares took great nerve and skill. For many of these missions the capabilities of the 'Lizzie' were unique: no other aeroplane could have flown into some of the makeshift 'airfields' in those conditions.

An interesting development was the 'tandem-wing' Lysander, in which a second wing was fitted at the tail and a rear gun turret was carried. Surprisingly enough, it flew well, but it was not ordered into production.

Before the first flight of the Lysander, test pilot Harald Penrose sat in the cockpit and felt the controls. The ailerons felt heavier in one direction than the other, while the elevator seemed too light.

It transpired they had been connected the wrong way round.

Later, one of his 'party pieces' was to take off apparently straight towards a building. In fact he was slightly to one side but to observers he seemed to fly just over it.

When a Turkish pilot arrived to evaluate the Lysander, Penrose was horrified to see him line up precisely towards the building. With skill and the Lysander's capabilities, he just cleared it.

Westland-Hill Pterodactyls
daring tail-less designs of the 1920s

Geoffrey Hill was a tail-less aeroplane enthusiast – such designs should have less drag and weight – who persuaded Westland to build as series of aircraft using his ideas.

The first of his 'Pterrible Pterodactyls' flew in 1928, and a series of progressively more advanced machines appeared over the next five years.

They achieved reasonable performance but suffered from the problem of all such designs in that era of difficult fore-and-aft control.

Test flying was eventful, to say the least, and take-offs comprised a series of bucking leaps over the grass until, with luck, a bump precipitated the machine into the air.

Test pilot Harald Penrose's confidence was not improved when turning the last version, Pterodactyl V, on the ground prior to its first take-off. He was alarmed to find the entire wing structure collapsing around him.

Development was eventually abandoned, but it is interesting how closely the first Pterodactyl resembles many modern microlights; in a sense Geoffrey Hill was too far ahead of his time, 20 years later he tried again, this time working with Shorts to design another research aircraft, the Short Sherpa.

Westland Wapiti
maid-of-all work and basis for first flight over Everest

The Wapiti was a general-purpose biplane with a single Bristol Jupiter engine. It made use of surplus DH9a parts wherever possible.

First flight was in 1927 and Wapitis were widely used for keeping troublesome tribesmen under control and army co-operation duties for some years. An improved version was called the Wallace, and one of these together with a development Westland biplane, the PV.3, made the first flight over Everest in 1933.

Both used modified Bristol Pegasus engines, heating and oxygen. Despite problems with intense cold and fickle weather over the mountain, the flight was successful and excellent film was taken.

> *After the first flight of the Wapiti, a draughtsman happened to measure the fuselage and to his astonishment found it 3 foot (1m) shorter than designed.*
>
> *A section had been accidentally omitted on assembly!*

Westland Whirlwind
impressive-looking but disappointing fighter

By the mid-1930s cannon armament (firing explosive shells) was becoming available for aircraft use and would clearly be more effective than machine-guns. It was thought impractical to mount such guns in the wings, although later both Hurricanes and Spitfires were modified to do so, so a twin-engine design was envisaged with four 20mm cannon in the nose.

Teddy Petter designed the Whirlwind as the smallest possible airframe to meet the specification. Unfortunately in his quest for compact size, he selected the Rolls-Royce Peregrine engine in preference to the larger Merlin. The Whirlwind was the sole application for the Peregrine so the engine suffered from lower priority than the all-important Merlin.

The Whirlwind was a most aggressive-looking machine, and its striking appearance led to its popular name of 'Crikey!', after a Shell advertisement of the time. Harald Penrose made the first flight in October 1938. The test flying was eventful, often due to Petter idiosyncracies of design like his insistence on routing the exhaust pipes through the fuel tanks, with almost inevitable result.

Production problems delayed the Whirlwind from operations until the end of 1940, so it missed the Battle of Britain. In service its performance was disappointing at high altitude but adequate at low level, so its duties were concentrated on ground attack missions. Only two squadrons flew Whirlwinds, and they were withdrawn in late 1943. Had it been a little larger and used Merlins, it might have been as successful as the Mosquito, and available earlier. Westland used the name Whirlwind again for the licence-built Sikorski S-55 helicopter.

Wright Flyer
the first powered aeroplane to fly

Wilbur and Orville Wright became interested in flying in the late 1890s. Crucially they (Wilbur was the prime mover at first) realised that it would not be enough just to become airborne: an aeroplane would need proper control.

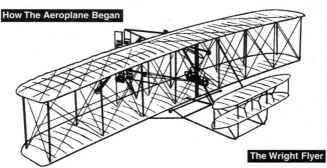

How The Aeroplane Began

The Wright Flyer

By studying bird flight, they recognised that shifting body weight would not be good enough, and devised their system of warping the wing-tips – similar in principle to ailerons. They also appreciated that one of the keys to success would be in learning piloting skills – most aspirants at the time seemed to have thought only about leaving the ground, not about how to handle the machine once in the air!

Gliding experiments started in 1900 at Kitty Hawk, North Carolina, the site being chosen for its consistent winds and low hills. Another attraction was its remoteness – early budding aviators were liable to be ridiculed.

Improved gliders followed over the next three seasons. The brothers were most methodical in testing different aerofoils, running thousands of tests in a wind-tunnel they had built. They also found a need to improve their control over the gliders, and in a piece of true inspiration hit upon the idea of a fin and moveable rudder, which in conjunction with wing-tip controls has been used as the standard method of control ever since.

In 1903 the brothers moved on to a powered machine, the first 'Flyer'. They built their own 12 hp engine and designed their own propellers, again using the wind-tunnel to decide their profile.

The first sustained, controlled, powered heavier-than-air flight occurred on 17th December 1903, when Orville managed 12 seconds and 120ft (37m). Later that day, Wilbur flew for 59 seconds.

The great day was somewhat spoilt when the Flyer blew over and was wrecked. It was restored and is displayed in the Smithsonian, Washington. The Wrights flew improved 'Flyers' over the next few years, but due to obsessive secrecy and later pre-occupation with guarding their patents, they eventually lost their commanding lead over other pioneers, and by the time of Wilbur's early death in 1912 the Flyers were already dated.

Soon afterwards Orville virtually severed all connection with aviation until his death in 1948.

THE FIRST "FLYER"

The historic Wright Flyer was a biplane with elevators mounted in front of the pilot, who lay on the lower wing. Fin and rudder were at the rear.

Angle of bank was controlled by the pilot shifting his hips in a cradle which twisted the wing-tips and also moved the rudder. The pilot worked the elevator with his hands. These arrangements made the Flyer tricky to fly.

The engine was a four-cylinder unit made by their mechanic, Charles Taylor. Historians argue whether it was wholly their own design or based on a car engine. It was the least efficient part of the Flyer but it served its purpose. Chains drove the two pusher propellers.

The original Flyer flew for under two minutes but earned its undisputed place in history.

Yakovlev fighters
leading supplier of Soviet combat aircraft

The Yak wartime fighters were the most numerous and among the best used by Russia during the Second World War. Alexander Yakovlev was reportedly inspired by the Spitfire to produce his clean-looking Yak-1, which together with the progressively developed -3, -7, and -9 played a crucial role in Soviet airpower. Some 37,000 are believed to have been built.

The first Russian jet fighter to enter service was the Yak-15, a straight-wing design based on the piston-powered Yak-3. It did not match contemporary Western fighters and for a time Yakovlev lost their pre-eminence to the MiG series.

Yakovlev have continued with advanced jet fighters, including the first Russian vertical take-off combat aeroplane, the Yak-36 'Forger', which appeared in the mid-1960s. Used as a carrier-borne fighter, like the Sea Harrier, it uses a single main engine and two lift jets. It is believed to have severely limited range.

Yakovlev have also built the highly successful Yak-18 and -50 aerobatic aircraft, which dominated international competitions for some years, and several airliners which have been widely used on Aeroflot services. The 1966 Yak-40 32-seat trijet looked at one time as though it would make substantial sales to Western airlines, and a licence was agreed to build it in America, but these hopes eventually collapsed.

> *Yakovlev's first light aircraft was the AIR-1, taking the initials of A.I. Rykov, a prominent politician of the time.*
>
> *Later Rykov fell from grace and was shot, whereupon Yakovlev swiftly changed the type number to Ya-1; it was rash to back losers in Stalin's Russia.*

Zeppelin-Staaken E.42/50
trend-setting airliner

This four-engine airliner, designed by Dr. Adolph Rohrbach, with metal construction and cantilever wing was about a decade ahead of its time when it flew in September 1920. Under restrictions limiting German aviation activities at the time it was destroyed under Allied orders, but Rohrbach's work inspired later all-metal airliners in the United States.

Zlins
aerobatic champions

The Czechoslovakian Zlin company was formed in 1935, oddly enough as a subsidiary of a shoe company. In the 1950s Zlin 226 Akrobats started to make their mark in aerobatic competitions, then in the 1960 World Aerobatic Championships they sensationally took the first four places.

The aerobatic champion himself, Ladislav Bezac, later flew his Zlin equally skillfully to defect with his family to the West, evading MiG jet fighters en route.

Zlins dominated world aerobatics for some years, and are still widely used by top pilots, but there is now stiffer competition from other types such as the American Pitts range, Russian Yakovlevs and now the impressive Sukhoi aerobatic machines.

It is perhaps fitting to end this book with one of the most extraordinary feats of flying in the annals of aviation: British aerobatic champion Neil Williams was practising in a Zlin 526A for the 1970 championships when a wing-spar failed. Immediately he rolled the aircraft inverted and stayed upside-down until just above the ground when he rolled again to land safely.

It is instructive to work out which way to roll to minimise the stress on the failed wing, and he had to decide instantly!

SIGNIFICANT DATES

17.12.1903* – first powered, controlled, sustained, heavier-than-air flight.

25.07.1909* – first aeroplane crossing of the English Channel.

21.01.1914* – first airline flights.

01.04.1918 – RAF formed.

28.05.1919 – first North Atlantic crossing completed.

15.06.1919 – first non-stop Atlantic crossing completed.

1919 (various dates claimed) – first international airline flights.

28.09.1924 – first round-the-world flight completed.

09.05.1926 – North Pole reached by air.

21.05.1927 – Charles Lindbergh's solo Atlantic flight completed.

09.06.1928 – first Pacific crossing completed.

28.11.1929 – South Pole reached.

06.11.1936 – Hurricane flies.

17.12.1935 – Douglas DC-3 (Dakota) flies.

06.03.1936 – Spitfire flies.

27.08.1939 – first jet flight, Heinkel 178.

15.05.1941 – first British jet flies, Gloster E28/39.

July 1944 – first jets in service, Meteor, Me 262, Arado 234.

20.09.1945 – first turboprop flight, Meteor with R-R Trents.

14.10.1947 – speed of sound exceeded, Bell X-1.

29.07.1950 – first turbine airline services, Viscount.

02.05.1952 – first jet passenger services, Comet.

20.11.1953 – Mach 2 exceeded, Douglas Skyrocket.

21.10.1960 – P1127 (Harrier predecessor) hovers.

21.12.1964 – first operational 'swing-wing' aircraft flies, F-111

22.01.1970 – Boeing 747 'Jumbo Jet' enters service.

21.01.1976 – Concorde enters service.

 * These events were preceded by equivalents in lighter-than-air flight – balloons or airships.

GLOSSARY

The use of technical terms, jargon, and abbreviations has been kept to a minimum, but a few are unavoidable and are listed below.

Aileron – small movable surfaces at the wingtips used for lateral control. Thus to bank the wings to the left, the aileron on the left wing is raised while that on the other wing is lowered.

Autogyro – a rotary-wing aircraft in which the rotors are driven by forward movement through the air. There is no drive from the engine to the rotors while cruising, although some could engage a drive for take-off only. The spelling 'autogiro' was a proprietary name for the Cierva company.

Axial Flow – a turbine engine layout in which the airflow proceeds in an essentially straight line through the compressor and turbine. It is the usual type today except in small engines.

BEA – British European Airways. The British airline which handled domestic and continental flights from 1946 until 1972, when it merged with BOAC to form British Airways.

BOAC – British Overseas Airways Corporation. The long-haul British airline formed in 1939 from a merger of Imperial Airways and British Airways. The latter name was resurrected for its successor in 1972.

Canard – a 'tail-first' layout or one using control surfaces forward of the wing.

Cantilever Wing – one without bracing wires or struts.

Centrifugal Flow – a turbine engine layout in which the compressor throws the air radially outwards before entering the combustion chamber. Most early British (but not German) engines were of this type.

Fly-by-Wire – controls operated electrically or by computer, with no mechanical link from the cockpit.

Mach Number – multiples of the speed of sound. Mach 1 is the speed of sound, Mach 2 is twice that, and so on.

RAF – Royal Air Force, formed as a separate service on 1st April, 1918.

RFC – Royal Flying Corps, the air branch of the army, superceded by the RAF in 1918.

RNAS – Royal Naval Air Service, the naval equivalent of the RFC, likewise merged into the RAF.

Turbojet – the simple form of jet engine in which all the airflow passes through the combustion chambers.

Turbofan – a jet engine in which part of the airflow is ducted around the combustion chambers and turbine. The term 'by-pass engine' was also used at one time.

Turboprop – a turbine engine driving a propeller.

USAF – United States Air Force.

INDEX

*Aircraft types are listed in this book by alphabetical order or
original manufacturers' names. This index is provided to help
readers find a type when they do not know who made it, or perhaps
know it under a later maker's name following company take-overs
or mergers.*

*Named aeroplanes only are listed. Where there is a type number
only, e.g. Boeing 707, it is almost invariably quoted with the
maker's name so listing is superfluous.*

A POCKET REFERENCE BOOK